THE

Pastor IN *Prayer*

BEING A CHOICE SELECTION OF

C. H. SPURGEON'S

SUNDAY MORNING PRAYERS

D1465096

AMBASSADOR

BELFAST ◆ **GREENVILLE**
NORTHERN IRELAND SOUTH CAROLINA

The Pastor in Prayer
C. H. Spurgeon

First Ambassador edition 1997
This edition 2001

ISBN   1   898787 89 1

Ambassador Publications
a division of
Ambassador Productions Ltd.,
Providence House
Ardenlee Street,
Belfast, BT6 8QJ
Northern Ireland
www.ambassador-productions.com

Emerald House Group Inc.
427 Wade Hampton Boulevard,
Greenville,
South Carolina 29609
United States of America
www.emeraldhouse.com

EDITOR'S PREFACE.

A MAN of faith and prayer, is an apt description of the late Pastor of the Tabernacle.

His faith was responsive to the Divine call and obedient to the Divine command : it grasped the promises of God and proved the secret of his strength for service and endurance.

Familiar with the mercy-seat, he sought for heavenly guidance and found in the exercise of prayer a well-spring of joy, and the inspiration for his ministry. Things not seen and eternal ever lay within the range of his soul's vision, and he lived as one who had business with eternity.

Mr. D. L. MOODY in commencing his first address in the Tabernacle, October 9th, 1892, pathetically recalled the time when he first entered the building, twenty-five years ago. He had come four thousand miles to hear Mr. Spurgeon. What impressed him most was not the praise, though he thought he had never heard such grand congregational singing ; it was not Mr. Spurgeon's exposition, fine though it was, nor even his sermon ; it was his prayer. He seemed to have such access to God that he could bring down the power from heaven; that was the great secret of his influence and his success.

The following selection of Mr. Spurgeon's Sunday morning prayers, reported verbatim, will be welcomed as a precious memorial of a life and ministry by which God was honoured, souls saved, believers edified, and "workers together with God" were encouraged in all holy service. They will furnish stimulus for the preacher in the pulpit and aids to devotion to saints in solitude.

The sermons to which the prayers were preludes, are published in the " Metropolitan Tabernacle Pulpit " : the hymns are contained in " Our Own Hymn Book."

SUBJECTS OF SERMONS

TO WHICH

THE PRAYERS WERE PRELUDES.

POETRY.

THE PERSONAL TOUCH.

"If I touch but his garments, I shall be made
whole."—*Mark* v. 28.

———

O LORD GOD, the great I AM, we do confess and cheerfully acknowledge that all come of Thee. Thou hast made us and not we ourselves, and the breath in our nostrils is kept there by Thy continued power. We owe our sustenance, our happiness, our advancement, our ripening, our very existence entirely unto Thee. We would bless Thee for all the mercies with which Thou dost surround us, for all things which our eyes see that are pleasant, which our ears hear that are agreeable, and for everything that maketh existence to be life. Especially do we own this dependence when we come to deal with spiritual things. O God, we are less than nothing in the spiritual world. We do feel this growingly, and yet even to feel this is beyond our power. Thy grace must give us even to know our need of grace. We are not willing to confess our own sinfulness until Thou dost show it to us. Though it stares us in the face our pride denies it, and our own inability is unperceived by us. We steal Thy power and call it our own till Thou dost

compel us to say that we have no strength in ourselves.
Now, Lord, would we acknowledge that all good must come
of Thee, through Jesus Christ by Thy Spirit, if ever we are
to receive it. And we come humbly, first of all acknowledg-
ing our many sins. How many they are we cannot
calculate, how black they are, how deep their ill-desert ;
yet we do confess that we have sinned ourselves into
hopeless misery, unless Thy free undeserved grace do
rescue us from it. Lord we thank Thee for any signs of
penitence—give us more of it. Lay us low before Thee
under a consciousness of our undeserving state. Let us
feel and mourn the atrocity of our guilt. O God we know
a tender heart must come from Thyself. By nature our
hearts are stony, and we are proud and self-righteous.

Help everyone here to make an acceptable confession
of sin, with much mourning, with much deep regret, with
much self-loathing, and with the absence of anything like
a pretence to merit or to excuse. Here we stand, Lord,
a company of publicans and sinners, with whom Jesus
deigns to sit down. Heal us, Emanuel ! Here we are
needing that healing. Good Physician, here is scope for
Thee ; come and manifest Thy healing power ! There
are many of us who have looked unto Jesus and are lightened, but we do confess that our faith was the gift of God.
We had never looked with these blear eyes of ours
to that dear cross, unless first the heavenly light had
shone, and the heavenly finger had taken the thick
scales away. We trace therefore our faith to that
same God who gave us life, and we ask now that we
may have more of it. Lord, maintain the faith Thou hast

created, strengthen it, let it be more and more simple. Deliver us from any sort of reliance upon ourselves, whatever shape that reliance might take, and let our faith in Thee become more childlike every day that we live ; for, O dear Saviour, there is room for the greatest faith to be exercised upon Thy blessed person and work. O God the most high and all-sufficient, there is room for the greatest confidence in Thee. O Divine Paraclete, the Holy Ghost, there is now sufficient room for the fullest faith in Thine operations. Grant us this faith. Oh work it in us now while at the same time we do confess that if we have it not it is our shame and sin. We make no excuse for unbelief, but confess it with detestation of it that we should ever have doubted the truthful, the mighty, the faithful God. Yet Lord, we shall fall into the like sin again, unless the grace that makes us know it to be sin shall help us to avoid it.

And now, Lord, we ask thee to accept of us this morning whatever offerings we can bring. We bring our hearts to Thee, full of love to Thee for what Thou hast done, full of gratitude, full of faith, full of hope, full of joy. We feel glad in the Lord. But we do confess that if there be anything acceptable in these our offerings, they are all first given us of Thee. No praise comes from us till first it is wrought in us, for

> " Every virtue we possess,
> And every victory won ;
> And every thought of holiness,
> Are thine, great God, alone."

Well may we lay those fruits at Thy feet that were grown in Thy garden, and that gold and silver and frankincense which Thou Thyself didst bestow, only first give us more !

Oh to love the Saviour with a passion that can never cool ;
Oh to believe in God with a confidence that can never
stagger !   Oh to hope in God with an expectation that
can never be dim !   Oh to delight in God with a holy
overflowing rejoicing that can never be stopped, so that
we might live to glorify God at the highest bent of our
powers, living with enthusiasm, burning, blazing, being
consumed with the indwelling God who worketh all
things in us according to His will ! Thus, Lord, would we
praise and pray at the same time. confess and acknowledge
our responsibilities, but also bless the free, the sovereign
grace that makes us what we are.   O God of the eternal
choice, O God of the ransom purchased on the tree,
O God of the effectual call, Father, Son and Spirit, our
adoration rises to heaven like the smoke from the altar of
incense.   Glory and honour and majesty and power and
dominion and might be unto the one only God, for ever
and ever, and all the redeemed by blood will say, Amen.

Look at this time, we beseech Thee, upon us as a
church and give us greater prosperity.   Add to us daily.
Knit and unite us together in love.   Pardon church sins.
Have mercy upon us that we do not more for thee.
Accept what we are enabled to do.   Qualify each one of
us to be vessels fit for the Master's use, then use each one
of us according to the measure of our capacity.   Wilt
Thou be pleased to bless the various works carried on by
the church ; may they all prosper.   Let our Sabbath
School especially be visited with the dew of heaven, and
the Schools that belong to us and are situated a little
distance, may they also have an abundant shower from the

Lord ; and may all the Sabbath Schools throughout the world be richly refreshed, and bring forth a great harvest for God.

Bless our College, O God; let every brother sent out be clothed with power, and may the many sons of this church that have been brought up at her side, preach with power to-day.   It is sweet to us to think of hundreds of voices of our sons this day declaring the name of Christ.   Blessed is the church that hath her quiver full of them, she shall speak with her adversaries in the gate ; but the Lord bless us in this thing also, for except Thou build the house they labour in vain that build it.   Bless our dear boys at the Orphanage.   We thank Thee for the conversion of many.   May they all be the children of God, and as Thou hast taken yet another away to Thyself, prepare any whom Thou dost intend to take.   We pray Thee spare their lives, but if at any time any must depart, may they go out of the world unto the Father.   May the Lord bless all the many works that are carried on by us, or rather which Thou dost carry on through our feeble instrumentality.

May our Colporteurs in going from house to house be graciously guided to speak a good word for Jesus.   And Lord bless us.   We live unto Thee; our one aim in life is to glorify Thee, Thou knowest.   For Thee we hope we would gladly die; ay, for Thee we will cheerfully labour while strength is given ; but, Oh, send prosperity, and not to us only, but to all workers for Jesus, to all missions in foreign lands, and missions in the heathendom at home.   Bless all Thy churches far and near, especially the many churches speaking our own language across the Atlantic, as well as in this land. The Lord send plenteous prosperity to all the hosts of His Israel. May Thy kingdom come ! And, Lord, gather in the unconverted : our prayers can never conclude without pleading for the dead in sin. Oh quicken them, Saviour ! and if any one here has a little daughter that lieth dead in sin, like Jairus may they plead with Jesus to come and lay His hand upon her that she may live. If we have any relatives unsaved, Lord, save them : save our servants, save our neighbours, save this great city, yea, let Thy kingdom come over the whole earth. Let the nations melt into one glorious empire beneath the sole sway of Jesus the Son of David and the Son of God. Come quickly, O Lord Jesus, even so, come quickly. Amen.

SERMON : No. 1382.   (November 4, 1877.)

SCRIPTURE : Matt. ix. 9-31.   HYMNS : 174, 415, 603.

II.

JESUS INTERCEDING FOR TRANSGRESSORS.

"He bare the sins of many, and made intercession for the transgressors."—*Isa.* liii. 12.

———

GRACIOUS GOD, we praise Thee with our whole hearts for the wondrous revelation of Thy love in Christ Jesus our Lord. We think every day of His passion, for all our hope lies in His death: but as often as we think upon it, we are still filled with astonishment that Thou shouldst so love the world as to give Thine only begotten Son, that whosoever believeth in Him should not perish but have everlasting life; that heaven's eternal darling should come to earth to be made a man, and in manhood's form to be despised and rejected of the very men whom He came to bless; and then should be made to bear the sin of many and to be numbered with the transgressors, and being found in that number to die a transgressor's death, a felon's death upon the gibbet of the cross. Oh this surpasses all belief if it had not indeed been actually so: and if the sure word of prophecy had not of old declared it, we could not have imagined it. It would have seemed blasphemy to have

suggested such a thought, yet Thou hast done it. Thy
grace has almost out-graced itself, Thy love has reached
its height : love to rebels ; so to love that even Thy Son
could not be spared.   O God, we are afflicted in our
hearts to think we do not love Thee more after such love
as this.   Oh, were there not a stone in our hearts we
should melt in love to Thee, we should account that
there was no thought fit to occupy the mind but this one
stupendous thought of God's love to us, and henceforth
this would be the master-key to our hearts, that should
unlock or lock them at Thy will—the great love wherewith
Thou hast loved us.   We lie in the very dust before Thee
in utter shame, to think that we have sometimes heard
this story without emotion and even told it without
tenderness.   The theme truly has never become stale to
us.   We can say in Thy presence that the story of Christ's
death still brings joy and makes our hearts to leap.   But
yet Lord, it never has affected us as we could have
expected it would.   Give us more tenderness of heart,
give us to feel the wounds of Jesus till they wound our
sins to death.   Give us to have a heart pierced even as
His was, with deep sympathy for His griefs, and an all-
consuming love for His blessed person.

We adore Thee, O Father, for Thy great love in the gift
of Jesus : we equally adore Thee most blessed Jesus, for
resigning Thy life for our sakes : and then we adore the
Blessed Spirit who has led us to know this mystery and
to put our trust in Jesus.   Unto the one God of Abraham,
Isaac, and Jacob, do we pay our reverent homage this
morning ; only we see Him yet more clearly than the

patriarchs of old did, for God in the face of Jesus Christ is seen in the clearest light that mortal eye can bear.

And now we have a prayer to put up to Thee, Great God, and it is this, that in us Thy dear Son may see some portion of the travail of His soul. Lord, let Him see a reward for His sufferings in all of us being repentant for sin, and trusting in God, and confessing His name. We fear there are among us this morning some who still indulge in the sins which brought Christ to death, some that still are trusting in their own righteousness and so are despising His, because if their's will suffice then His were superfluous. O God, we beseech Thee bring men away from all their false trusts to rest in the great sacrifice of Thy dear Son. Let not one person here be so callous to the merit of Christ as not to love Him, or so indifferent to the efficacy of His blood as not to desire to be cleansed in it. Oh bring every one of us now to believe in Jesus Christ with our whole heart unto eternal life, that so the thousands in this Tabernacle may belong to Jesus, that He may have a portion with the great. But even those who have believed in Christ have need to put up the same prayer. Our Lord and Master, Redeemer and Saviour, come and take entire possession of us. We own Thy right, but Thou must take by force what Thou hast purchased, or Thou wilt never have it. By force of arms, the arms must be those of love, wilt Thou capture our wilful, wayward spirit. Come and divide the spoil with the strong in us we pray Thee. Take every faculty and use it, overpower and sanctify it. Every moment of our time help us to employ for Thee, every breath may we

breathe out to Thine honour.   We feel that there is uncon-
quered territory in our nature yet.   Subdue, Lord, we
beseech Thee our corruptions, cast them out, and in our
spirit rule and conquer.   There set up thine eternal
throne—

> " Wean our heart from every creature
> Thee to love and Thee alone."

We do pray this with our whole hearts ; and assist, us we
pray Thee most blessed Redeemer, to show forth Thy
praises in our lives.   Sanctify us in our households.
May we go in and out before Thee shewing the name
and nature of Christ.   Help us in our business, that in all
we do among our fellow men we may act as Christ
would have us act.   Strengthen us in secret ; there may
we be mighty in prayer.   Guard us in public, that neither
in act nor word we may slip away from Thee.   Above all,
cast cords of love around our hearts.   Oh hold us
Saviour, never let us go.   Suffer no professed Christian
here ever to violate the loyalty of his obedience to his
King.   May those dear wounds of His have more sway
over us than ever silver sceptre had over the subjects of
earthly princes.   May we feel that if He drank for us
the vinegar and gall, whatever cup He sets before us we
will cheerfully drink.   Rule us, Saviour, rule us, we beseech
Thee.   And let no believer here violate the chastity of his
heart to the Beloved of his soul.   O Jesus, let us love
Thee so intensely, that whatever else there may be of
loving relationship, still this may cover all and swallow up
all.   Oh to be wholly Christ's !   We do mourn that we
cannot reach to this—that in the secret of our hearts every

devil should be cast out, every demon driven to its deep, every sin made hateful, every thought of sin made loathsome to us, until only pure desires and inward longings after perfect holiness shall predominate in our nature. O God, let the scourge still be used to drive out the buyers and sellers: we would not ask to have them spared, but let the temple be the Lord's, seeing He hath built it and hath cleansed it with His blood. Bless at this time very graciously the church to which we belong. Let us in this place know the power of prayer to-day and to-morrow: especially pour out upon the members of this church an intense spirit of supplication. May we agonize to-morrow for the glory of God, and to-day also, and let it not depart from us so long as we live. Send us, Lord, a mighty ground swell of intense desire for the glory of God, and may these Thy servants banded together in church fellowship recognise their sweet obligations to their dying Lord, and determine that the prayers of the church shall go up before Him like sweet perfume.

Lord, convert our friends that still remain unsaved. Oh mighty power of God, let none come into this house even accidentally and casually without receiving some devout impression. May the Spirit of God work mightily by our ministry and the ministration of all His servants now present, whether in the Sabbath School, or in the streets, or in the lodging houses, or from door to door, or when they privately speak to individuals. Oh, glorify Thyself in us. Dear Saviour, we pray Thee come and mark us all distinctly with the blood mark as being wholly Thine, and henceforth may we say with Paul, " Let no man trouble me, for I bear in my body the marks of the Lord Jesus." As we have been buried with Thee by baptism into death, so would we be dead to all the world and only live for Christ. God grant it may be so, and we will glorify Thee in life and death and for ever.

As Thou hast bidden us pray for all men, so do we now especially pray for our beloved country. May every blessing rest upon this favoured isle. Upon the Queen let Thy mercies always descend. Keep this land in peace we beseech Thee, and as for all other lands may peace yet reign. May oppression in every place be broken to shivers, and may truth and righteousness win the day. Break in pieces the power of Antichrist we pray Thee, and of the false prophet, and let the idols fall from their thrones, and may the Lord God Omnipotent yet reign, even Jesus, King of kings and Lord of lords. We ask it all in His name. Amen.

SERMON : No. 1385.   (November 18, 1877.)

SCRIPTURE : Isa. liii.   HYMNS : 327, 412, 329.

III.

GOD'S THOUGHTS AND WAYS FAR ABOVE OURS.

" For my thoughts are not your thoughts, neither are your ways my ways, saith the Lord. For as the heavens are higher than the earth, so are my ways higher than your ways, and my thoughts than your thoughts."—Isa. lv. 8, 9.

————

O GOD, most high and glorious, the thought of Thine infinite serenity has often cheered us, for we are toiling and moiling, troubled and distressed here below beneath the moon, but Thou sittest for ever in perfect happiness. Thy designs cause Thee no care or fear, for Thou wilt surely carry them out. Thy purposes stand fast as the eternal hills : Thy power knows no bound, Thy goodness no stint. Thou bringest order out of confusion, and our defeats are but Thy victories. We sow in tears, but Thou dost see us reap in joy. Our everlasting felicity is present to Thee, even while groans and mourning are our present lot. Glory be to the Lord most high, who sitteth on the clouds, who sitteth King for ever and ever. Our hearts rejoice to hear the gladsome tidings that the Lord reigneth. Let His kingdom be established over the sons of men, for His kingdom must come, and of it there will be no end. Behold, we come to Thy throne this morning bearing about with us a body of sin and death, and consequently much of sin, and much of care, and it may be much of sorrow; but we would be unburdened at Thy mercy-seat now. As for our cares we are ashamed that we have them, seeing Thou carest for us. We have trusted Thee now for many years, and Thy faithfulness has never been under suspicion, nor Thy love a matter of question. We therefore leave every concern about our families or about ourselves, about our business, or about our souls, entirely with our God. And as for our sin, we bless Thee for a sight of the precious blood of Jesus : when Thou seest it Thou dost pass over us. No angel of justice smites where once the blood is sprinkled. Oh, let us have a sight of the blood of Jesus, too, and rest because Thou hast for ever put away our sin, because we believe in Jesus. Thus, Lord, help us to stand before Thee, entering into Thy rest as we enter into Thy presence ; and may this be a time of peace wherein the peace of God which passeth all understanding, shall keep the hearts and minds of His people through Christ Jesus.

Still, Lord, we have a burden which we must now lay before Thee, and ask Thee to help us in it. We mourn over the condition of Thy church, for on every side as we look around we see men endeavouring to undermine the doctrines of the everlasting Gospel. Time was when a man was famous for lifting up his axe upon the trees of the forest, but now they with axes break down the carved work of Thy sanctuary, they despoil Thy truth. There is scarce a single doctrine of Thy word which the wise men among us do not deny. Yea, and those that pretend to be the ministers of the gospel are amongst the first to speak against it, and to denounce it, and to sanction licence to sin because Thou wilt no more punish it, and to declare that Jesus Christ is not Thy Son. O Lord God, our heart often sinks within us ; we are apt to wish to lay our hand upon the ark to steady it, for the oxen shake it; but we know it is in Thy hand, and having spread the case before Thee we leave it there. Many a Rabshakeh's letter have we read of late : behold we bring it into the sanctuary and spread it before the Lord. O Lord our God, rebuke the unbelief, rebuke the scepticisms of those who assail both Thee and Thy Christ, and the gospel of Thy truth.

And we would ask Thee to do it thus if it please Thee : revive deep spirituality in the hearts of Thine own children. Oh that we might live so near to the great Shepherd as to be familiar with His voice, to know its tones, that so a stranger we may not follow, for we know not the voice of strangers. If it were possible they would deceive even the very elect, and how shall Thine elect be kept from their deceptions but by abiding in the truth and walking in the power of the Holy Spirit. Oh revive Thy church we pray Thee in this respect ! Give to those who know Thee intenser faith in the eternal verities, burning into us by experience the things which we do know ; may they be beyond all question to us. And may we never be ashamed to glory in the good old way, the way the fathers trod, the way which leads to heaven and to God. May we not be ashamed to vindicate it, and to bear reproach; for Thy gospel has of old been to the Jews a stumbling-block, and to the Greeks foolishness, and so we expect it ever to be a stumbling-block to those who go after the way of superstition, and also to be foolishness to the wise men of the world.   O God, again confuse the knowledge of men by what they think to be the foolishness of the gospel.   Again let it be seen that the foolishness of God is wiser than men, and the weakness of God is stronger than men.   O Jesus, Son of the Highest, we know that the truth is powerful, because Thou art the soul of it—the very essence of it.   Put Thy life into it we pray Thee.   May the eternal spirit go with every word which God-sent ministers shall proclaim, and may the Lord grant that as the mists fly before the sun and the clouds before the wind, so error and superstition may be driven away by the rising of the Sun of Righteousness in all the glory of His brightness.

We have also to bring before Thee another burden, and that is the godlessness of this present age.   It is not alone the wise men but, behold, the men that know not seek not after God.   O Lord, the multitude delight in sin. Drunkenness defiles our city, and filthy words are heard on every side.   Be not wrath with this nation, we beseech Thee.   It has been entrusted with wondrous privileges. Forgive it and have mercy upon its aggravated sin.   Lay not its heavy responsibilities to its charge, but let this nation be saved.   We pray for it as we are in duty bound to do, and as our love constrains us to do.   Oh let the masses of the people yet come to seek after Christ, or by some means, by all means, by every means, may the ears of men be reached and then their hearts be touched.   May they hear, that their souls may live; and may the Lord who in everlasting covenant sets forth His Son, glorify Him in the midst of the nations. Let all the nations know the Christ of God. Our Father, we pray Thee help the few, valiant few, that press forward into the dense area of the enemy. Help them to fight valiantly ! May these pioneers of the Christian host in mission lands be increased in number, may they be kept in good heart, may they have confidence in God, and may the Lord send the day of victory much sooner than our feeble faith has dared to hope.

But, Lord, we have yet another burden—it is that we ourselves do not love Thee as we should, that oftentimes we grow lukewarm and chill, and doubt creeps over us, and unbelief mars our confidence, and we sin and forget our God. O Lord help us ! Pardon is not enough, we want sanctification. We beseech Thee let the weeds that grow in the seed plot of our soul be cut up by the roots. We do want to serve Thee. We long that every thought we think, and word we say or write, should be all for Thee. We would lead consecrated lives, for we are persuaded that we only live as we live unto God, that aught else is but trifling. Oh to be taken up as offerings wholly to be consumed upon the altar of the Lord, joyfully ascending to Him in every outgoing of our life. Now this morning be pleased to refresh us. Draw nigh unto us, Thou gracious God ; it is only Thy presence that can make us happy, holy, devout or strong. Shadow us now with Thy wings, cover us with Thy feathers, and under Thy wings may we trust. May we follow very near unto Thee, and so feel the quickening warmth, the joy which only Thy nearness can bring. If any in Thy presence this morning are unsaved, oh save them now. Do grant that the service of this morning may bring such glad tidings to their ear, that their heart shall leap at the sound of it, and they shall return unto God, who will abundantly pardon. Bless every preacher of the Word to-day, and all Sabbath schools, classes of young men and women, all tract distributing and street preaching, and preaching in the theatres, and every form of holy service. Accept the prayers and praises of Thy people. Receive them even from the sick beds of those detained at home. Let not one of Thy mourners, the weary watchers of the night, be kept without a smile from God. The Lord bless us now, and all His chosen people. Our soul crieth out for it. Break, O everlasting morning, break o'er the dark hills! Let our eyes behold Thee, and till the day break and the shadows flee away, abide with us, O our Beloved abide with us now. Amen.

SERMON : No. 1387. (December 2, 1877.)

SCRIPTURE : Isa. lv.   HYMNS : 36, (Song i.), 103, 202.

IV.

EJACULATORY PRAYER.

"Then the king said unto him, For what dost thou make request ;. So I prayed to the God of heaven."—*Neh.* ii. 4.

———

O LORD, our God, how excellent is Thy name in all the earth! Some of us have to thank Thee for many mercies bestowed. We thank Thee for them, for we feel that we are entirely in Thy hands in all respects. Others of us have been brought very low, bruised full sore, but having a little strength remaining, we desire to praise and bless the Giver of every gift. Thou art good when Thou givest, and Thou art good when Thou takest away. Thou art good when the night gathers heavy about us. Thou art good when the sun shineth and gladdeneth our pathway. Thou art always good and doest good,. and blessed be the name of the Lord from the rising of the sun unto the going down thereof, and through the night watches let His praise be still celebrated. In the recollection of all that Thou hast done for us Thy people, we are filled with amazement as well as with gratitude,.

that Thou shouldst have loved us before the foundation
of the world, that sovereign love should have pitched upon
us poor unworthy ones, that Thou shouldst so love us as
to redeem us with the blood of Jesus and give the only
Begotten to die for unworthy creatures like to us; that
Thou shouldst love us notwithstanding our sins and
transgressions, that Thou shouldst love us despite the
hardness of our hearts and the rebellion of our nature.
It is strange, it surpasses belief at times, yet do we know
it to be so.   And since the hour when we knew Thy love
and learned to say Abba, Father, we do confess we have
been unworthy still.   We have but little felt Thy goodness;
we have often acted very ungratefully, very distrustfully.
But Lord, Thou hast not changed, but still doth Thy faithfulness abound to Thy servants; for which again we can only
say, Blessed be the name of the Lord.

Especially would we make mention of the goodness of
the Lord during another year.   Each believer here has
trodden a different pathway : to some it has been a very
smooth road, to others a very rough climb : to some a
deep descent into the valley of sorrow and humiliation.
But Thou hast led Thy people by a right way.   With all
the twisting of the wilderness march, we are persuaded
that when Thou leadest us about, still we go the nearest
way.   Thou knowest best, and oftentimes to retreat is to
advance, and to be beaten back is to make surest head-
way.   We would again in the recollection of the whole
year, whatever it may have been, lift up the song of
grateful praise, raise another stone of help to record the
loving-kindness of our God.

And now do we hoist sail and draw up anchor to sail into another year. O Thou blessed Pilot of the future as of the past, we are so happy to leave all to Thee; but in leaving all to Thee we have one wish, and it is that Thou wouldst in the next year glorify the Father's name in us more than in any other year of our lives. Perhaps this may involve deeper trial, but let it be if we can glorify God. Perhaps this may involve the being cast aside from the service that we love; but we would prefer to be laid aside if we could glorify Thee the better. Perhaps this may involve the ending of all life's pleasant work and the being taken home—well, Thy children make no sort of stipulations with their God, but this one prayer ascends from all true hearts this morning, " Father, glorify Thy name." Wilt Thou glorify Thyself, great Father, by making us more holy. Purge us every day, we beseech Thee, from the selfishness that clings to us. Deliver us also from the fear of man, from the love of approbation so far as these might lead us astray. Help us to be resolute and self-contained to do, and think, and speak the right at all times. Give us great love to our fellow men. May we love them so that we could die for them if need be.

Above all, blessed Jesus, our Reedemer, let Thy love to us fire us with love to Thee. Stamp Thy dear image on our hearts, and let us never wander from the path of complete obedience to Thy will. Here we stand, asking to be washed again in the open fountain that every sin may be put away; but also begging to be washed in the water " from the riven side that flows," that every wrong

desire, every base aspiration, everything contrary to the mind of God may be utterly taken away from us. We beseech Thee strengthen Thy servants for the battles of another year. Give them courage for all the trials, give them grace for all the joys. Help us to be a holy and a happy people ! Let the redeemed of the Lord speak well of His name, and whatever their distress may be at times yet over all may they lift up notes of perpetual joy, glorying in the name of the Lord their God.

We ask Thee, O God, at this time to revive religion in our land. Oh that Thou wouldst be pleased to speak by the Holy Ghost that the gospel's power may be known : there be many that run away from the truth ; Lord, hold us fast to it, bind us to it. May there be a people found in this place, and throughout this land, that will abide by the doctrines of the gospel, come what may. May we not be ashamed to be old fashioned and to be thought fanatical. May we not wish to be thought cultured, nor aim to keep abreast of the times. May we be side by side with Thee, O bleeding Saviour ; and be content to be rejected, be willing to take up unpopular truth, and to hold fast despised teachings of sacred writ even to the end. Oh make us faithful, faithful unto death.

And now Lord, bless this people, this our beloved church. Thou hast been very gracious to us ; be gracious to us still. Oh that we had health and strength to labour here as our heart desireth : may it please Thee yet to give us these ! But if not, use what there is of us till the last is gone, and be pleased ever to find some one or other to go in and out before this people, to feed them with knowledge and understanding. "Father, glorify Thy name."

We ask Thee once more that Thou wouldst, by some means, cause peace to be re-established throughout the earth. Grant that this nation may not be drawn into war. We have been foolish once over it, grant that we may not be so again, but Oh, let Thy Kingdom come without the use of the sword. Oh angel of war, wilt thou not rest! Oh sword of the Lord, put thyself into thy scabbard and be still; for the sake of the great Prince of Peace we ask it. Amen.

SERMON: No. 1390. (September 9, 1887.)

SCRIPTURE: Neh. i. and ii. 1-8. HYMNS: 181, 636, 978.

IN CHRIST.

—o—

In Christ I feel the heart of God
  Throbbing from heaven through earth:
Life stirs again within the clod:
  Renewed in beauteous birth.
The soul springs up, a flower of prayer,
Breathing his breath out on the air.

In Christ I touch the hand of God,
  From His pure height reached down,
By blessed ways before untrod,
  To lift us to our crown ;—
Victory that only perfect is
Through loving sacrifice, like His.

Holding His hand, my steadied feet
  May walk the air, the seas ;
On life and death His smile falls sweet,—
  Lights up all mysteries:
Stranger nor exile can I be
In new worlds where He leadeth me.

Not my Christ only : He is ours ;
  Humanity's close bond ;
Key to its vast unopened powers,
  Dream of our dreams beyond.—
What yet we shall be, none can tell ;
Now are we His, and all is well.

Lucy Larcom.

V.

THE DAY OF SALVATION.

"Behold, now is the accepted time, behold, now is the day of salvation."—2 *Cor.* vi. 2.

O GOD, Thou art our exceeding joy. The very singing of Thy praises lifts our heart upward: when we can join in the solemn psalm or the sacred hymn, our heart doth leap within us. And when Thy name is glorified, when we see sinners glorifying the name of Jesus, when we look forward to the brighter days when myriads shall flock to the Crucified: above all, when we contemplate His final triumph, then is our heart very restful and our spirit rejoiceth in God our Saviour. What a fountain of delight Thou art, and how richly hast Thou promised to bless the men that delight themselves in God. Thou hast said, "Delight thyself also in the Lord, and He shall give thee the desire of thine heart." Dost Thou reward us for being delighted? Oh pleasant duty, which hath appended to it so divine a promise. Shall we have the desire of our heart when our heart finds all its desire in Thee? Oh blessed Lord, Thou dost indeed meet them that work righteousness and that rejoice in Thy ways; and Thou fillest Thy people with good things, so that their

youth is renewed like the eagles'. We pray Thee help
us who know Thee, to glorify Thee. We have known
Thee from our youth, some of us, and hitherto have we
declared Thy wondrous works. Oh may there never be
in our heart, and above all may there never come from
our lips, or in our life, anything that might dishonour
Thee. Oh let us die a thousand deaths sooner than ever
dishonour Thy hallowed name. This is dearer to us than
the apple of our eye. We have loved the habitation of
Thy house, and the place where Thine honour dwelleth.
Gather not our soul with sinners, nor our lives with cruel
men ; but let us be helped, even to the end, to follow the
Lamb whithersoever He goeth, even if it be to Gethsemane
and Calvary. Oh to be perfect in heart towards the
Lord ! Our lives are faulty ; we see much to grieve over ;
but we would have our whole heart towards Thy statutes ;
and we bless Thee that so it is, for our heart is in Thy
ways, and we are willing to spend and to be spent for
Thee. Reservation would we not make to the very
slightest, but lay ourselves out for Thine honour only, for
by us and in us, Father glorify Thy name.

Look down upon the great assemblies of this morning
all over the world, and let Thine eye of tenderness rest
here. Thou seest here many that love Thee—may we
love Thee more ! Thou seest many that live by the life
of God—oh life of God live in us to the full ! Thou seest
also, we fear, some that are declining from Thy ways, in
whom grace is but a flickering light. Lord, trim the
lamps, bring back the wanderers, for there is no joy but
in God. And perhaps, nay we fear it must be so, that

Thou seest in this throng, ungodly ones, careless and indifferent. Oh sword of the Lord, pierce them through, that carelessness may be slain, that their souls may live. Oh Thou who art as a polished shaft hidden in the quiver of the eternal, go forth to-day to smite to the heart the proud, the self-righteous, and those that will not stoop to ask mercy at Thy hands : but as for the humble and the contrite, look upon them ; the broken-hearted and the heavy-laden do Thou relieve, and such as have no helper do Thou succour. Bring up the sinner from the prison house, let the lawful captive be delivered. Let the mighty God of Jacob lead forth His elect, as once He did out of Pharaoh's bondage. The Red Sea is already divided that they may march through it. The Lord save multitudes—He knoweth them that are His. Accomplish their number and let Jesus so be rewarded, though Israel be not gathered.

Oh Lord, we ask ourselves for strength to bear and to do. Some of us would ask, if it were Thy will, restoration to health ; but Thy will be done. Others would ask deliverance out of trouble—again, Thy will be done. Some would come before Thee with conscious guilt, and ask for a new application of the precious blood. We had better all ask it, let us all have it. O God bless this church and people more and more. How richly thou hast blessed them ! When we look back upon past years, what hath God wrought! Shalt thou be without our song ? Even when we are not as we would be, shall our voice, if it be cracked and broken, still be silent ? No, if every harp-string shall be broken but one, that one shall still resound the love of Jesus, and the glory of God. Long as we live we will bless Thy name, our King, our God of love ; for there is none like Thee. "Whom have we in heaven but Thee, and there is none upon earth that we desire beside Thee." Our soul is clean divorced from all earth's good, and married to the Christ of God for ever. By bonds that never can be snapped we are one with Him, and who shall separate us from His love ?

The Lord be pleased to reveal Himself to His servants. Oh for the uplifting of the veil, for the drawing near of the people that are made glad by the blood, for the speaking of God unto the soul, and the speaking of our soul unto God. Oh for converse with the Eternal, for such fellowship as they may have who are raised up together with Christ, and made to sit in the heavenlies with Him. Oh Saviour, grant us a glimpse of Thy great love. One flash of Thine eye is brighter than the noonday. One word from Thy lips will be sweeter to us and more full of music, than the harps of angels. Grant it to every one of Thy children all over the world, both to the sick and to the dying. Oh how gloriously will they die !

And now Lord, we ask Thee to bless our country at this time, and by Thy great and infinite mercy preserve us we beseech Thee from war. Oh that peace may reign yet all over the world, but let not this nation intermeddle and be as one that taketh a dog by the ear, but may there be wisdom given where we fear folly, and strength given where wisdom reigns. The Lord grant that wars may utterly cease unto the ends of the earth. Oh make a way we pray Thee, for the progress of Christianity, of civilization, of liberty, of everything that is honest and of good repute. May Thy kingdom come, and Thy will be done, on earth, as it is in heaven, for Thine is the Kingdom, the power and the glory, for ever and ever.   Amen.

SERMON : No. 1394.   (January 13, 1878.)

SCRIPTURE : Isa. xlix.   HYMNS : 241, 239, 406.

CHRIST IS ALL.

—o—

OH, the bitter shame and sorrow,
    That a time could ever be
When I let the Saviour's pity
Plead in vain, and proudly answered,
" All of self, and none of Thee."

·Yet He found me.   I beheld Him
    Bleeding on the accursed tree,
Heard Him pray, " Forgive them, Father ! "
And my wistful heart said faintly,
" Some of self, and some of Thee."

Day by day His tender mercy,
    Healing, helping, full and free,
Sweet and strong, and ah ! so patient,
Brought me lower, while I whispered,
" Less of self, and more of Thee ! "

Higher than the highest heavens,
    Deeper than the deepest sea,
Lord, Thy love at last hath conquered ;
Grant me now my soul's desire,—
" None of self, and all of Thee !

MONOD.

VI.

SITTING OVER AGAINST THE SEPULCHRE.

" And there was Mary Magdalene, and the other Mary, sitting over against the sepulchre."—*Matt.* xxvii. 6.

———

MOST glorious Lord God, it is marvellous in our eyes that Thou shouldst become incarnate, that Thy Son should take our flesh upon Him. It surprises us greatly that the Lord of Life should condescend to die, and that the incorruptible One should be laid in the grave. We are full of loving gratitude, we are also full of adoring wonder. When we have stood at the sepulchre and looked into it and thought of Jesus having lain there, when we have seen it open and knew that it was empty, we bless Thy name that even He died and was buried, and magnify Thee that He is risen again from the dead. These great facts concerning our divine Lord are the foundation of our confidence in Him. We bless Thee that they have been attested by such four-fold witness, and yet further that afterwards He appeared alive to so large a number of those who knew Him that the fact of His rising from the dead might never be questioned again. We do not question it, our hearts devoutly believe the fact, but Lord we want by Thy Holy Spirit to know the facts in their living power. We wish that we might have fellowship with our Lord, who is our Head, in all this. Oh that we might know how to die

with Him, and to live with Him in newness of life. O
God we do rejoice that the old man was crucified with
Him. We would daily mortify the flesh with its affections
and lusts. We wish to be to the world, to sin, to selfishness as dead and buried men; as dead men, out of mind,
so would we be. Oh that no faculty might hear the voice
of the charmer when it charms us towards sin! may we be
delivered from the mere power to obey the lusts of the
flesh and the temptations of the devil. May grace so
sanctify us that we may reckon ourselves to be dead indeed
unto sin, but alive unto God through Jesus Christ our
Lord. O God we have too much of the ill alive about us.
Go on to crucify it: let it die and, painful and lingering
though the death may be, may we reckon the thing to be
dead, because it is crucified, and never treat it as though
it were a living thing to be fed and to have provision made
for it: but let it die and let it be buried. May those of
us who bear in their body the marks of the Lord Jesus be
solemnly concerned that our baptism should be no fiction,
but that we should be really baptized into the death of
Christ with all the fulness of the deadening power that is
about the sacred burial by fellowship with Him. And, O
Lord, give us more and more to have the new life, yea,
and to have it more abundantly, for this is one of the
objects of His coming. May the new life always rule us,
may we walk by its power, may we have strength through
its influence, may we be elevated by its energies, may we
be indeed entirely subjugated as to our own entire
manhood to the control of the Holy Spirit through the
new-born life. We do pant for this.

We ask especially on this Lord's Day that we may be in the Spirit and so may be in the fulness of the quickening power. May we do nothing after the dead manner of formality. May there be no dead hymn, nor dead prayer. Lord, give the preacher life. Oh give the hearers life. Oh may this be living worship this morning, the bowing not of heads alone, but of hearts, and the closing not alone of the eyes to things that can be seen, but the closing of the eyelids of the thought to everything worldly.

O Lord, imprison us in the grave of Christ to-day, that within those sacred walls we may find a chamber where our Lord shall manifest Himself to us, as He doth not unto the world.

A spring shut up, a fountain sealed art Thou O Christ to us, and we would be such to Thee ; a garden enclosed for our Beloved, wherein He may take His delights. Our soul shall sing for joy, "I am my beloved's, and my beloved is mine ; he feedeth among the lilies."

Oh ! for a day's release from every care ! Now break the bands of our yoke. And Oh that we could live above care in the week-days too, casting all our care on Him who careth for us, and leaving all in those wise hands that rule the world, and can well rule our mean affairs. To-day, gracious Lord, reproach Thy children and comfort them, also rebuke and reprove as may seem good unto Thee; but Oh, sanctify us for the skies, and prepare us for the place which Thou art preparing for us. The Lord be very mindful of all his sick servants at home, of any that are under depression of spirit, and especially of such as are near to die

Oh be very gracious to all Thy children under tempta
tion, and if any are in very sharp trial, and are also
conscious of having brought it upon themselves, which
makes the trial worse than ever, yet of Thy mercy do
Thou let the fulness of the power of Thy grace be manifest
in them, that in the ages to come they may, with all saints
declare the exceeding riches of Thy power and love in
Christ Jesus.

And now, Lord, bless the unconverted that come into
this house to-day, or into any other place of worship.   Be
pleased to save them ; let the eternal purpose be fulfilled
in many to-day   .Oh bring home Thy prodigal children,
and let such as are coming home be met by the loving
Father, and may such as have come home have a feast of
fat things to-day.   May elder brethren to-day be made
better tempered, be made more into sympathy with the
great Father !   May there be blessings all round to-day
for all of us, and so may we together bless and magnify
Thine august and sacred name.   O Thou one God of
Israel, whom we worship, let others worship whom they
may ; the God of Abraham, of Isaac, and of Jacob is our
God for ever and ever, and we worship Thee Oh Jehovah
Elohim, in the name of Jesus Christ Thine only begotten
Son.   Amen.

SERMON : 1404.   (March 24, 1878.)

SCRIPTURE : Matt. xxvii., 44-61.   Mark xv., 42-47.
Luke xxii. 50-56. John xix. 38-42. Rom. vi. 1-13.
HYMNS : 909, 832, 844.

VII.

THE REASON WHY MANY CANNOT FIND REST.

" Submit yourselves therefore to God. Resist the devil, and he
will flee from you. Draw nigh to God, and he will draw nigh to
you. Cleanse your hands, ye sinners ; and purify your hearts, ye
double-minded. Be afflicted, and mourn, and weep ; let your
laughter be turned to mourning, and your joy to heaviness.
Humble yourselves in the sight of the Lord, and he shall lift
you up."—*Jas.* iv. 7-10.

———

PERMIT us, gracious Father, to come very near to
Thee. May the drawings of the Divine Spirit now
sweetly attract us to God ; and most blessed Jesus, fulfil
Thine office as Mediator, bring us now near to God by
Thy precious blood. Oh for the power to pray aright
this morning ! May Thy servant have it largely that he
may be able to lead all this people, by the power of the
Spirit, close to the mercy-seat.

First would we adore and bless and magnify our God ;
not only O God for what Thou art to us, but for what
Thou art in Thyself, for Thou art incomparably glorious.
In Thee, all perfections shine. Through the rebellion of
our flesh we cannot delight ourselves in Thy ways, because

they are hard and afflictive apparently; yet we do delight in Thee, and we will at all times rest our souls in the excellence and goodness and lovingkindness of the Most High.   As Thou hast revealed Thyself in Christ Jesus, Thou art now become to Thy people the object of inexpressible delight.   Thou hast bidden us delight in Thee, promising to give us the desire of our hearts.   We trust we can, many of us, truly say that Thou art our exceeding joy; the thought of God doth to our soul exceeding pleasure bring.   Our soul exulteth in her God: He is our God and we will extol Him, He is our fathers' God and we will glorify Him.

But, Lord, we do confess that our nature is at enmity with Thee.   The fallen corrupt nature of Adam has revolted and gone aside from God; and though we hope that by Thy free grace Thou hast renewed us, yet the old rebellions come up at times, and the evil nature urgeth us still to oppose Thee.   Therefore our prayer this morning is that we may not only extol Thee with our words, as we do now; but by the entire submission of our hearts in loyal reverence to Thee, we may pay Thee the truest homage.   But, Lord, lest we should not have done this, or thinking that we have done so, should still have failed, we will make this the burden of our morning prayer.   A large number of us have put on Christ by open confession of His name.   Oh Searcher of hearts, are we really in Christ?   Have we been by His spirit begotten again? Wilt Thou be pleased to search our hearts, that this question may be put beyond all suspicion.   Help us to be very diligent in self-examination, observing whether our spirit be the spirit of Thy children, whether our griefs be the griefs that tear repenting hearts, whether our joys are the joys of faith or the delusions of presumption. May we make severe trial of ourselves, often and often putting ourselves into the balances of the sanctuary, to see whether we be full weight or no. One thing we hope we can say with confidence, that our trust is stayed where Thou wouldst have it stayed, even in the work, the blood, the righteousness, the person of Thy dear Son. We have no confidence but in Christ, this we know; but Lord, if this be a true confidence it will work by love and purify the soul. Oh that there might be the sweet results of faith about our secret character and public life. We do sin, the Lord grant we may never leave off grieving because of sin, never may we be contented with ourselves, never fancy that we have reached a point where we may rest and be thankful, and that there is nothing more for us to do in seeking to be more than conquerors of ourselves. As we have read the charge of Thy word against that unruly member, the tongue: as we have heard Thy servant James rebuking our envy and other evil spirits that are within us, we do feel humbled under Thy hand, and our prayer is, Lord, kill our envy, Lord, help us to command our tongue, grant us grace to be holy: may we be kind and gentle towards our fellow men, having that fruit of the Spirit, which follows upon purity, even peace. Oh that we might live for Thee and not for self. Slay self we pray Thee, gracious God, whenever there is a selfish, angry disposition about us; help us to trample it out, as men put out sparks lest a fire should arise therefrom.

Oh to be Christly ! We do desire to live on earth the
life of Jesus—sent into the world by Him as He was sent
into the world by the Father. We would closely copy all
His acts, words, and spirit ; for so only are we saved, when
we are saved from the power of sin and transformed into
the likeness of Christ. Let no drunkard here imagine
that his life ought to be spent in a selfish endeavour to
save himself from the flames of hell ; but may he rather
reckon that the grand object is to be saved from the power
of sin, and to be consecrated unto God, and to live unto
the glory of the most High. Oh Lord, we do fear that
selfishness even enters into our most holy things ; we
mar and spoil our prayers, and preachings, and teachings,
with the unwashed hands with which we go about them.
Oh that Thou wouldst make us clean we pray Thee ; while
we thus pray to Thee, we do also know that believing in
Christ we are clean ; we thank Thee we do not doubt His
justifying power. While we are now crying to Him to be
sanctified, may we not doubt His power to sanctify ; but
while crying, "O wretched man that I am, who shall deliver
me from the body of this death," as well we may, we do
nevertheless shout exultingly, "Thanks be unto God who
giveth us the victory through Jesus Christ our Lord."

And now we beseech Thee, look upon some who are
seeking salvation, but do not find it ; who hear the simple
gospel but somehow cannot enter into its rest. We know
that something hinders—Satan hinders. There may be in
the heart of seekers here, attachment to a favourite sin.
Oh deliver them from that fascination. There may be
still some holding fast to evil associations, some predomi-

nance of evil passions. Oh God help penitent souls to
come to Thee, asking to be delivered from sin in every
shape, from the sugar of sin as well as from the gall of
sin. Oh make the soul of the seeker to be weary till he
is delivered from corruption. May there be none here
that shall fancifully seek after a pretended salvation, which
will leave them as they are, but may they know that Jesus
saves His people from their sins; and, oh, that with
self-loathing, and deep contrition, and earnest heart
searching, souls may come to Thee again and cast
themselves before Thy face, trusting in Jesus, and crying
out to be delivered from sin; and may this be the day of
deliverance. Oh that at this very hour, while we are
trying to preach, Thou mayest raise up of these stones
children unto Abraham. Men that seem naked and cold
as stones, quicken by the mighty Spirit this very day; and
may they be led to yield themselves unto God, and
their members instruments of righteousness. The Lord
grant it, and we will bless His name.

Lord, save us all, not only now, but in that day. So
as by fire perhaps some of us will be saved, but we had
rather pray that thou wouldst minister unto us an entrance
abundantly into the Kingdom of our Lord and Saviour
Jesus Christ.

We have many things to ask of Thee, but Thou
knowest, without our use of words. Give to all before
Thee, and to all Thy people everywhere, exactly what
Thou seest they need. We pray for the revival of the
Church of God, for help to be given this day to all
preachers, and teachers, and seekers after the souls of

others. We pray Thee, Lord, to add to Thy church daily of such as shall be saved. With our whole heart many of us at least do pray Thee to bless our country, and spare it from the horrible evils of war. O God of peace, send us peace always, by all means. Sword of the Lord rest and be quiet now ; and may the gospel with its benign influences spread over all nations, till there shall be no selfish clutching, no rapacious grasping at territories, no oppression of one race by another ; but may the laws of the King of Peace be universally proclaimed, and obeyed even by those who perhaps yield not their hearts to His sway ; for we do know, great King, that whilst Thou hast a special kingdom in Thy people, yet the Lord hath given Thee power over all flesh ; and we pray this may be recognised, and we may see it. Thy kingdom come, O Jesus ; may Thy kingdom come, Thy Father's kingdom ; and let His will be done on earth as it is in heaven ; for Thine is the kingdom and the power and the glory for ever and ever. Amen.

SERMON : No. 1408. (April 7, 1878.)

SCRIPTURE : James iii., iv. 1-12. HYMNS : 907, 641, 119 (Song ii.).

VIII.

THE CONQUEST OF SIN.

"For sin shall not have dominion over you: for ye are not under the law, but under grace."—*Rom.* vi. 14.

———

GLORIOUS Lord God, our inmost hearts worship Thee; for Thou art high above the heavens, and yet Thou humblest Thyself to behold the things that are in heaven and that are on earth. And in Thy condescension Thou hast regard to the very lowest of mankind. Many of us can sing "He hath regarded my low estate"; for Thou dost raise the poor out of the dust, and the needy out of the dunghill, that Thou mayest set them among princes, even the princes of the people. Who is a God like unto Thee: Hallelujah! our praises shall never cease: from the rising of the sun unto the going down of the same, and all through the night watches, the Lord's name is to be praised.

Our Father, for that is the sweetest title by which we can address Thee, we pray Thee save us entirely from sin. There are many in Thy presence who are resting in the peace which comes of justification by faith. We know that we are righteous through the righteousness of another, even Jesus Christ; but we pant and pine for personal likeness to Thyself. If Thou be our Father, then upon

every child of Thine should be the Father's image
impressed : so let it be. We beseech Thee, Lord, to enable
us to recognize our death to sin ; and when it tempts us
may we be deaf to the voice of the charmer with the
deafness of death; and when it would use our members
as instruments of unrighteousness, may we be quite
incapable thereof with the incapacity of death.   O God,
deliver us we pray Thee from the invasion of sin, as well
as from the dominion of it.   Grant us to walk as Christ
walked ; in His newness of life may we live—may the
life in the flesh be a life of faith upon the Son of God
who loved us and gave Himself for us ; and may it be a
life of love, and consecration of burning zeal for God ; a
life of pure holiness ; such a life as the incarnate God
Himself has lived among the sons of men.

We lament that in the body of this death there is much
that we abhor.   We are tempted to indolence at times, and
though busy in the world we become spiritually idle.
Also, we are tempted to envy others because they excel
us, and we mourn to confess the meanness of our spirit in
this matter ; and also we have to lament our pride.   We
have nothing to be proud of ; the lowest place is ours ; but
Lord, we often conceive ourselves to be something when
we are nothing.   We pray Thee forgive all these vices of
our nature ; but at the same time kill them, for we hate
ourselves to think we should fall into such evils.   Especially
have mercy upon us for our unbelief.   Thou hast given
us proof of Thine existence, and of Thy love to us, and of
Thy care over us : especially hast Thou given us Thine
only begotten Son, best pledge of love.   And yet we

acknowledge that we do doubt. Unbelief comes into the soul. We are quite ashamed of this. We could lie in the very dust to think it should be so. Lord, have mercy upon us; but also help us to be strong in faith in the future, giving glory to God.

We must sorrowfully also lament our hearts, how they wander. If Thou givest us a blessing we begin to idolize it. How often do we set our hearts upon children, upon some beloved object, or upon wealth or upon honour. Somehow or other, this spiritual adultery too often comes upon us, and the chastity of our hearts towards our God is violated. Be pleased to forgive us in this thing also.

"Take this poor heart and let it be,
For ever closed to all but Thee"—

a spring shut up, a fountain sealed. Let the whole heart be Christ's alone, and never stray again.

Yet we do bless Thee this morning that we can pray in this fashion, for there was a time when it never struck us that there was much amiss with us, when sin was no plague to us; when we lived even in outward sin with but slight accusation of conscience, and certainly without any pain at heart. Thou knowest, Lord, that sin is our greatest curse; we would sooner suffer anything than sin, at least when we are in our right mind we feel so. O God, deliver us from sin! At the very thought of its coming near to us we cry, "O wretched man that I am, who shall deliver me;" and we only find comfort in the blessed truth that Thou givest us the victory through Jesus Christ, our Lord. Let that victory be very apparent, may it be very clear to our own consciousness, very much displayed in our lives. O God, help us to live towards Thee in all devotion, confidence, obedience, resignation and simple childlike trust. Help us to love Thee with all our heart and soul and mind. Enable us also to live to our fellow-men according to Thy word, loving our neighbour as ourselves. Save us from all unneighbourly tempers, all hard thoughts, all slanderous words. Deliver us from bearing any anger in our heart: from everything that is ungenerous or unkind do Thou save us, and let the law of love be written on the fleshy tablets of our renewed heart, and be carried out in all the thoughts and words and acts of our lives. Especially help us to master our tongue, for if that be bridled the whole body will be manageable. Keep us, O God, when we are in company, and equally preserve us when we are in secret. Help us to keep the door of our lips; and grant that when that door is opened there may not come out of it sweet waters and bitter: may we not both bless and curse, but may we speak that which is good to edification, and may our speech be also seasoned with salt.

Thus would we cry unto Thee after holiness. Thou knowest we do not expect to be saved by it; but we do look upon it as salvation to be saved from sin, to be delivered from corruption; to be emancipated from the bondage of the evil is the great thought of our spirit, and we look forward to heaven with this as one of its highest felicities, that we shall be without fault before the throne of God, and that nothing that defileth shall ever enter there. O Lamb of God, by whom we have been redeemed from sin and washed from uncleanness, wilt Thou graciously daily wash our feet that we may be clean every whit, and may enter in through the gates into the city, and be among those of whom it is written—"They shall walk with Me in white for they are worthy."

And at this hour, which is an hour of grace, we would ask Thee to help any of Thy children who are under bondage. If they have lost their hope, if their faith has become weak, if their love burns low, Lord renew the faith of Thy people like that of the eagles; and let them mount up with eagles and rise above their doubts, their deadness, and their care.

Should any of Thy servants be in deep trouble, wilt Thou grant them grace to glory in tribulation also, because it worketh patience, experience, and hope. And may the Lord grant to all his tried and troubled ones, beauty for ashes, the oil of joy for mourning, and the garment of praise for the spirit of heaviness.

Prosper Thy universal church. Send the preaching of the pure gospel again to the world. Silence the voices of those that are spreading infidelity and superstition: and may the day come when every pulpit shall resound with the pure gospel of Jesus Christ, and His people shall again return to their allegiance to the faith—the faith once delivered to the saints, never to swerve again.

O God, suffer us to intercede with Thee a moment for our unconverted ones. Give us to feel great sorrow and heaviness of heart for those who, as yet, are far off from God: Lord, bring them in. O God, awaken the careless and frivolous—there may be such here this morning, who have never given any solemn consideration to the matters of their soul. May they be awakened and aroused to-day; and while we set forth the way of salvation by grace, may they feel their need of it and be willing to accept it; and may the Lord save them this day.

May any that are anxious, but are missing the mark, looking to themselves instead of to Christ, learn the way of life and run in it. Save them, O God; yea, save this people. Let all within the Tabernacle walls to-day be within the Temple gates above at the last. May every congregation of the faithful everywhere be under the Divine blessing.

Bless our country, we pray Thee : and we lift up again the voice of earnest prayer that peace may not be broken. Oh, let not bloodshed break forth in the midst of the continent; but may it please Thee to send wisdom to the councillors of all nations, that by some means such a dreadful calamity may be avoided; and may He come who will end all danger of war, even the Prince of Peace Himself, in whose days shall the righteous flourish and abundance of peace so long as the moon endureth. The Lord hear us now; and forgive, and answer, and bless, according to His riches in glory by Christ Jesus : and unto Israel's one God revealed to us in the Trinity of Mystic Persons, Father, Son, and Holy Ghost, be glory by Christ Jesus. Amen, and Amen.

SERMON : No. 1410. (April 21, 1878.)

SCRIPTURE : Rom. v., vi.   HYMNS : 911, 647, 64

IX.

TRUE PRAYER—HEART PRAYER.

" For thou, O Lord of hosts, God of Israel, hast revealed to thy servant, saying, I will build thee an house : therefore hath thy servant found in his heart to pray this prayer unto thee."—
2 *Sam.* vii. 27.

———

OH Lord, our song reminds us of what we were, and we would begin our praise by the acknowledgment of our natural condition ; we would remember the miry clay and the rock whence we were hewn, for we were " by nature children of wrath even as others." Well do we remember when we felt this, and when the bitterness and gall were in our mouths, of which we had to drink both day and night. How heavy was the load of sin! all our thoughts were engrossed with that sense of pressure and of dread. We looked on the right hand and there was none, and on the left and we found no helper ; but then Thou didst Thyself deliver us by leading us to cast a faith-look to the Divine, only begotten, and crucified Son. At this moment vividly is it upon our recollection how Thou didst bring us up out of the " horrible pit :" we remember now the new song which Thou didst put into our mouths

as we found our feet fast on the rock and our goings
established. It is long since then with some of us, but
all the way has been strewn with mercies, and we desire
this morning to record, " Bless the Lord, oh my soul, and
forget not all His benefits."

We thank Thee now in the retrospect for the trials
which we have endured. Some of us have been brought
very low with physical pain and mental weariness, and
others have been sore smitten with bereavement, losses
and crosses, and persecutions, but there is not one out of
all our trials which we could have afforded to have been
without. No, Lord, all has been ordered well, there was
a need-be for every twig of the rod, and we desire now to
thank Thee that we can see in looking back, how all
things have even now worked together for good, though
we know we cannot see the end as yet.

Oh Thou good God, Thou blessed God, like David
we would fain sit down before Thee in silence and wait
awhile, for our words when we do use them are totally
inadequate to the expression of what we feel, much more
of what we ought to feel concerning Thy goodness and
Thy loving kindness ; yet we will bless Thy name with such
language as we have. Jehovah, our God, let others
worship whom they will and seek after what object of love
they please, this God is our God for ever and ever, He
shall be our guide even unto death. Father, Son, and
Holy Spirit, the Triune God of Israel, we express most
solemnly the reverence we feel for Thee ; and render to
Thee our humble adoration as we acknowledge Thee to
be the One and only God, by whom the heavens and the

earth were made, by whom all things consist, the Redeemer of Thy people, their Father and their Friend, for ever and ever ! All our hearts worship Thee, Oh Thou glorious Lord !

And truly since we have received so many mercies at Thy hand, we do feel that Thou wilt never forsake us nor in any darkness which may be in our path in the future, wilt Thou desert Thine own. Thou hast done too much for us to desert us now. We have cost Thee so much—Oh wondrous price that Thou hast paid for us—and Thou hast spent so much of wise thought, and gracious act upon us, that we are persuaded Thou wilt go through with the work which Thy wisdom has undertaken. But give us faith to believe this : when the stormy times come, let us not doubt, but what our helmsman will bring us to the desired haven. Though winds and waves assault our keel, may we still find perfect peace and rest in the thought that He who is in the hinder part of the ship is Master of winds and waves. Comfort Thy children this morning, great Father, if any of them are in doubt just now ; and bring them all into an assured confidence and perfect restfulness in the Lord their God.

Next, we would humbly entreat of Thee that we may each one be permitted to do some great service for Thee before we go hence : we do not mean great in the wisdom of our fellows, but let it be all that we can do. If we cannot build a house for Thee, yet have we set our hearts upon doing something ; and if it be Thy will, direct our minds to what it shall be, lest our minds should not be Thy mind : but let not one of us be barren or unfruitful.

If we have indeed been redeemed by the blood of Christ, may we reckon that we must live to Him; may the love of Christ constrain us, and may something come of our lives that shall be a blessing to the sons of men, ere we go hence.

And our Father, while we offer this prayer, we will also pray with a deep gratitude for all Thy mercies: may they take possession of all our hearts that, as when David sat in his house of cedar he "magnified the Lord," so may we also whenever things go smoothly with us. Lord, may the gratitude we feel prompt us to say again "what shall I render to the Lord for all His benefits towards me." Make every child of thine here to be every day serving Thee; and serving Thee so that heaven's work may begin below, and something of heaven's pleasure may be enjoyed even now. But Lord, while we work for Thee, always keep us sitting at the feet of Jesus. Let our faith never wander away from the simplicity of its confidence in Him. Let our motive never be anything but His glory; may our hearts be taken up with His love, and our thoughts perpetually engaged about His person. Let us choose the good part which shall not be taken away: that if we serve with Martha we may also sit with Mary.

Let this church, Lord, receive a fresh annointing of the Holy Ghost, that all its members may be spending themselves for the Master. Wilt Thou quicken, we pray Thee, every agency; In all our Sabbath schools, may there be no lack of teachers, may our young friends find it a delight to be teaching the little ones; may there be even a superabundance of workers in this department.

Let not anything flag to which the church has set her hand. Prosper us in the education of our young men for the ministry! bless us, we pray Thee, with our dear orphan boys : may they, all of them, be saved in the Lord with an everlasting salvation. Remember our colporteurs scattered about this country, and prosper them in their going from house to house with the Word of God, and may they be great soul-winners, all of them, that the Lord's name may be glorified.

And all the thousand and one things which constitute the activities of the churches at large, do Thou bless and prosper them so far as they are according to Thy mind ; and may it please Thee to give to the churches prayer in proportion to activity, and faith in proportion to zeal. O Lord ! visit Thy church at this time, which is a time of peril, and in Thy mercy revive among us the love of the pure gospel of Jesus Christ. Rebuke, we pray Thee, those who with their philosophy and vain deceit would mar and spoil the gospel of Jesus Christ. Grant that in all deliberations of any part of Thy church, which concern this great and grievous and crying evil, there may be decision and wisdom and help given, that all may be done and ordered to Thy glory.

Bless our nation, Lord, we pray Thee, and let the spirit of Christianity permeate it, enter into the high places, and flow down even to its darkest dens. And, we beseech Thee, let us have peace ; may nothing happen to break it, may it be established on a firm and judicious footing, and for many a year may no sound of trumpet, or noise of cannon be heard throughout the whole earth.

Let the people praise Thee, O God, and learn war no
more ! Let all the nations be blessed ! May the gospel
of Christ Jesus penetrate into the remotest regions, and
where it is known may the power of it be felt far more.

Bless our brethren across the sea of another land, but
who with the same tongue worship our Lord in spirit and
in truth, and our brethren on the southern side of the
globe, and all the scattered saints in every nation ; visit
them with the bedewing of the Holy Ghost, and make the
gardens of the Lord amidst the desert to be green, and
blossom as the rose. Now help us this morning, give to
every one a sense of pardoned sin : forgive us, O Father,
for Christ's sake ! Give to each one of us also sanctifying
power, that we may be cleansed from the influence of
guilt. Give power in the delivery of the gospel. May
the truth sink into the soul, and may this be a good and
happy, devout and beneficial occasion to all of us here
gathered. We ask it for Jesus' sake. Amen.

SERMON : No. 1412.   (May 5, 1878.)

SCRIPTURE : 2 Sam. vii.

X.

DISTINCTION AND DIFFERENCE.

"Ye have wearied the Lord with your words. Yet ye say, Wherein have we wearied him? When ye say, Every one that doeth evil is good in the sight of the Lord, and he delighteth in them; or, Where is the God of judgment?"

"Then shall ye return, and discern between the righteous and the wicked, between him that serveth God and him that serveth him not."—*Mal.* ii. 17 ; iii. 18.

———

TRULY God is good to Israel, even to such as are of a clean heart. Thy people desire to set their seal to this, and to acknowledge that Thou art overflowing goodness. O Thou blessed God, Thou hast remembered both our temporal and our spiritual wants ; Thou hast lifted us up from the gates of the grave, delivered our soul from death, our eyes from tears, and our feet from falling. Thou hast dealt well with Thy servants, O Lord, according to Thy Word. There is none like unto the God of Jeshurun, there is none that dealeth so bountifully; for as high as the heavens are above the earth, so high are His thoughts above our thoughts and His ways above our ways. Our soul, therefore, blesseth God the Lord, and all that is in us is stirred up His holy. name to magnify and bless. " Bless the Lord " is the utterance

of our inmost soul this morning ; " from the rising of the
sun unto the going down of the same let the Lord's
name be praised."

And now, Lord, Thou wilt listen to us while we
confess before Thee how unworthy we have been of all
Thy goodness ; for we are a sinful generation, even as our
fathers were.   We have sinned times without number,
and even those of us who are Thy people, and have been
born into Thy house, we have even more than others to
mourn over our sin, for Thou hast made us more sensible
of it, and we have sinned against greater light, which we
do sorrowfully confess.   Our sins of pride, of unbelief,
of hasty judgment of Thy providence, our neglect of
searching into Thy mind in the Word, our neglect of
possessing Thy mind in our daily life, our transgressions
and our shortcomings make against us a great list of
accusations.   But we bless Thee that they will not stand
as accusations, for, behold, none can lay anything to the
charge of Thy people, seeing all was laid on Him upon
whom the transgression of Thy people was laid of old by
Thine own hand; and now, washed in His precious
blood, and clothed in His matchless righteousness, we
know that despite our faults we stand accepted in the
Beloved, for which again we bless Thee.   Deep down in
our hearts shall the song begin in humiliation of spirit
because of our offences, but it shall rise to the very heights
of heaven while with exultation we behold how we are
" raised up together and made to sit in the heavenly
places," and are presented in Christ Jesus " without spot
or wrinkle or any such thing."

Lord, we desire this morning to contemplate with admiration Thy ways toward us. Thou hast put some of us into the furnace. There is no child of Thine but knows something of the heat of the furnace, and we perceive that Thou art as a refiner unto us, and that the fire is meant to consume our dross and tin, therefore do we thank Thee for it. For all the acts of discipline to which we are subject we would praise the wisdom and the love of our divine Father. Thou wouldst not have us live in sin; sin is much worse than furnace work. All the trial in the world is not so hard to carry as a sense of sin. Lord, if Thou dost give us choice to keep our sins and to live in pleasure, or to have them burnt away with trial, we will say to Thee, Lord, give us the sanctified affliction, but deliver us from all the influences of sin, from every evil habit, from all the accretions of former sin, all the ore that is mixed with the precious metal, everything that diminishes the brightness of Thy grace in us, everything that keeps Thee from taking delight in us, take it away, we beseech Thee: and if this life is to be to Thy people the crucible and the burning heat, even to a white heat, so let it be, so long as Thou dost sit at the furnace mouth to watch the ore that nothing should be lost. Oh, blessed God, help any of Thy children that are in the midst of the heat now. Let them see the Lord sitting near and watching, and let them feel perfectly at ease, because in His hands all things must be well.

And gracious God, we pray Thee, work in us according to the chapter we have been reading such a holy love to Thee, that we may render to Thee all that

we have. We have sometimes said in our soul: "Take
not tithe, but take Thou all." Keep us true to this.
May we feel that we are "not our own but bought with
a price," and let this be no sentiment which ought to
have power over us, but a real force which doth constrain
us, because "we thus judge that if one died for all, then
all died, and that He died for all, that they which live
should not henceforth live unto themselves, but unto Him
that died for them and rose again." We do pray for
grace that we may spend all our time, every faculty, and
all that we possess in glorifying our Lord and Master
amongst the sons of men in

> "Works which perfect saints above
> And holy angels cannot do."

This morning be pleased to accept the thanksgivings
of Thy servants for any special mercies received, and
especially of one who begs us to thank Thee for Thy
grace and mercy extended to her and the fifty little ones
with whom she was about to cross the sea. They went
through fire and through water, but still Thou didst
preserve them, and we pray God speed them on their way
to the distant land, and bless that sister who spends her
life in gathering the arabs of the street that she may take
them to a land where they will be well cared for. Oh
Lord, prosper her and all others that in any way seek the
good of the poor and needy.

Bless, we pray Thee, all city missionaries, all visitors
from house to house, all those who seek to reclaim fallen
women, or waifs and strays among the children. Let the
philanthropic work that is done in our city, ever be under

Thine eye, and be upheld by Thy gracious hand. Our ragged schools, and especially our Sabbath schools, do Thou look upon with favour, and grant them ever to be a nursery for the Church of God. And the Lord bless all that in any way seek to make known the savour of the name of Jesus. Oh, give the humblest tongue that tells of Christ to speak with fire, and where the multitudes are gathered together, there give fervour and earnestness, sincerity and depth of power to bring sinners to Jesus. "Let the people praise Thee, O God, yea, let all the people Thee !"

Let our great cities be swept clean of vice and infidelity and superstition. Deliver our country villages and hamlets from the drunkenness and ignorance in which they dwell. Let the whole earth behold the brightness of the coming of the Lord. Let Jesus Christ reign from pole to pole until He Himself shall come openly and manifestly to take to Himself His great power, and all the kingdoms surrender themselves into His hands.

And now, Father, save any in this house who remain unreconciled to their God. Touch now with Thy sacred finger some careless heart that may be using even the House of God as a place for the gratification of curiosity, desiring no spiritual gift whatsoever, yet wilt Thou be pleased to lay Thy hand upon that heart and make it feel that God is near, and may conscience say : " Be ye sure of this, that the kingdom of God hath come nigh unto you." And, oh, that there might not be the power to put aside that kingdom, but may the conscience now be so touched and girded with strength that the will may submit, and the judgment yield, and the affections bow, that God may reign over many a heart which hitherto has been a rebellious province of His domain. Again we say, " Let the people praise Thee, O God, yea, let all the people praise Thee ! " Save this assembly this day ; let every one that is within these walls, or shall be here, be saved. And now may the good seed drop into furrows that shall welcome it, and from it may there spring a harvest to Thy glory, O Thou ever blessed, unto whose name be honour, world without end, through Christ Jesus our Lord. Amen.

SERMON : No. 1415. (May 19, 1878.)

SCRIPTURE: Mal. ii. 17 ; iii.   HYMNS: 885, 714, 728.

XI.

TAKE FAST HOLD.

"Take fast hold of instruction; let her not go: keep her; for she is thy life."—*Prov.* iv. 13.

———

BLESSED God, our heart doth praise Thee, our inmost soul exults in Thy name, for the Lord is good, and His mercy endureth for ever. Thy people praise Thee, O God, for all that Thou hast been unto them, and we can each one set forth Thy worthy praise by reason of our personal experience of Thy goodness. Thou hast dealt well with Thy servants, O Lord, according unto Thy word. We bless Thee for teaching us from our youth, for some of us have known Thee, even from our childhood, and Thy word was precious to us even in our earlier days, when, like young Samuel, we were spoken to of the Lord. Now Thou hast borne and carried us these years in the wilderness with unchanging love and goodness, and there be some in Thy presence this morning who know that even to hoar hairs Thou art He—Thou hast made and Thou dost carry; Thou dost not forsake the work of Thine own hands. "Thy mercy endureth for ever," and let Thy praise endure for ever also.

O Lord, we would cling to Thee more firmly than ever we have done : we would say, " Return unto Thy rest, O my soul, for the Lord hath dealt bountifully with thee, for Thou hast delivered my soul from death, mine eyes from tears and my feet from falling." We would this morning " take the cup of salvation and call upon the name of the Lord." We would "pay our vows unto the Lord now, in the courts of the Lord's house, in the midst of all His people." Blessed be the name of the Lord, we have been brought low, but the Lord hath helped us ; we have oftentimes wandered, but He has restored us ; we have been tried, but He has preserved us ; yea, we have found His paths to be " paths of pleasantness " and all the ways of His wisdom to be " ways of peace." We bear our willing witness to the testimony of the Lord, we set our seal that " He is true " and we cry again " Bind the sacrifice with cords, even with cords unto the horns of the altar." From henceforth let no man trouble us, for we "bear in our body the marks of the Lord Jesus." We are His branded servants henceforth and for ever. Our ear is nailed to our Master's door-post, to go no more out for ever.

And now, Lord, we beseech Thee, hear the voice of our cry. Thy people would first of all ask Thee to deepen in them all the good works of Thy grace. We do repent of sin—give us a deeper repentance ! May we have a horror of it, may we dread the very approach of it, may we chastely flee from it and resolve, with sacred jealousy, that our hearts shall be for the Lord alone. We have faith in Jesus, blessed be Thy name, but Oh strengthen and deepen that faith ! May He be all in all to us ; may we never look elsewhere for ground of rest, but abide in Him with an unwavering, immutable confidence, that the Christ of God cannot fail nor be discouraged, but must for ever be the salvation of His people. We trust we can say also that we love the Lord, but Oh that we loved Him more! Let this blessed flame feed on the very marrow of our bones. May the zeal of Thine house consume us; may we feel that we love the Lord with all our heart, with all our mind, with all our soul, with all our strength, and hence may there be about our life a special consecration, an immovable dedication unto the Lord alone.

O Lord Jesus, deepen in us our knowledge of Thee. Thou hast made the first lines of Thy likeness upon our character; go on with this work of sacred art till we shall be like Thee in all respects. We wish that we had greater power in private prayer, that we were oftener wrestling with the covenant angel. We would that the Word of God were more sweet to us, more intensely precious, that we had a deeper hunger and thirst after it. Oh that our knowledge of the truth were more clear and our grip of it more steadfast. Teach us, O Lord, to know the reason of the hope that is in us, and to be able to defend the faith against all comers. Plough deep in us, great Lord, and let the roots of Thy grace strike into the roots of our being, until it shall be no longer I that live, but " Christ that lives in me."

Holiness also of life we crave after. Grant that our speech, our thoughts, our actions, may all be holiness, and "holiness unto the Lord." We know that there be some that seek after moral virtue apart from God. Let

us not be of their kind, but may our desire be that everything should be done as unto the Lord, for Thou hast
said, " Walk before Me, and be thou perfect." Help us
so to do, to have no master but our God, no law but His
will, no delight but Himself. Oh, take these hearts, most
glorious Lord, and keep them, for "out of them are the
issues of life," and let us be the instruments in Thy hand,
by daily vigilance, of keeping our hearts, lest in heart we
go astray from the Lord our God. Until life's latest hour
may we keep the sacred pledges of our early youth. We
do remember when we were baptized into the sacred
Name—Oh never may we dishonour that sacred ordinance
by which we declared that we were dead to the world and
buried with Christ. Some of us do remember our early
covenant with God, when we made over to Him ourselves
and all that we had. Oh, in life's last hour when we bow
ourselves for weakness, may it be to bless that sacred bond
and to " enter into the joy of our Lord." And if Thou
hast taught us anything since then, if Thou hast given us
any virtue or any praise, may we hear Thee say, " Hold
fast that which thou hast, that no man take thy crown."
Oh let no brother or sister become distinguished in grace
and then decline, let none bear fruit and afterwards become
barren, but may our path " shine more and more unto the
perfect day." It is this our spirit craveth after with strong
desire, that the whole of our life from the commencement
with Christ to its ending with our being with Christ, may
glorify and bring help to His Church.

And now hear Thou us again while we cry unto Thee.
Our chief desire is for Thy cause in the earth. We are

often very heavy about it. The days seem to us to be neither dark nor light, but mingled; oh that the element of light might overcome the darkness ! We do pray Thee, raise up in these days a race of men that shall know the gospel and hold it fast. We do feel that we have so much superficial religion, so much profession without true possession to back it up. Oh, Lord, may our churches be built with precious stones, and not with wood, hay, and stubble. May we ourselves so know the gospel that no one can beat us out of it; may we so hold it that our faces shall be like flints against the errors of the age ; so practice it that our lives shall be an argument that none can answer, for the power of the gospel of Jesus. And with this be pleased to grant to Thy churches more power over the sons of men. Oh Lord, make Thy ministers throughout all the world to be more fruitful in soul winning. Let us not rest without sowing the good seed beside all waters. Forgive us our coldness and indifference ; forgive us that we sleep as do others, for it is high time for us to awake out of sleep. Oh Lord, do help us to live while we live; shake us clear of these cerements, these grave clothes, which cling to us ; say to us, most blessed Jesus, what Thou saidst concerning Lazarus of old, " Loose him, and let him go." May we get right away from the old death and the old lethargy, and live under the best conditions of life, diligently serving God. Convert the nations, we pray Thee ! Help our dear brethren who stand far out in the thick heathen darkness, like lone sentinels ; let them bear their witness well, and may the day come when the

Christian church shall become a missionary church, when all over the world those that love Christ shall be determined that He shall conquer. Thou hast not yet made the church "terrible as an army with banners": would God she were. May those days of Christian earnestness come to us, and then shall we look for the latter day of glory.

And now, Father, save any in this house that remain unconverted. May this day be the day of their salvation. We would most earnestly entreat that some word may drop into the most careless heart; and this prayer especially, convert this day in this house of prayer, if it may please Thee, some that shall be very earnest Christians in years to come; take hold to-day of some whom Thou hast ordained to be like Paul, who shall be missionaries to the ends of the earth! Take hold of some that are specially set against Thee, some that are very bold spirits even in sin, thorough-hearted in their wickedness—convert such now! Say unto them, "See I have made thee a chosen vessel to bear my name unto the Gentiles," and may there come such power with it that they may not be disobedient unto the heavenly vision. Thy Church needs such men. Oh that such were brought out to-day! We put it up as a prayer to be registered in heaven, and we mean to look for its answer, that Thou wouldst to-day take hold of some men that shall become afterwards leaders in the church of God, this day striking them down with the sense of sin and leading them to Christ.

The Lord bless our country. God save the Queen. Keep us in peace, we beseech Thee and in times of congress and deliberation may there sit in the council chamber One higher than the kings of the earth, and greater than the ambassadors thereof. Oh that long-continued peace might happen to this poor earth, for its wounds are many. Behold, how all things languish for the lack of peace—the Lord send it. Quicken trade and commerce, remove the complaining that is now heard in our streets. Kindly consider us in the matter of the weather, that the harvests may not be spoiled, and bless the people, O Lord. Let the people praise Thee, and "then shall the earth yield her increase." The Lord grant all this, with the forgiveness of sin, the acceptance of our person, and assist us ever to live to His glory, for Jesu's sake. Amen.

SERMON : No. 1418. (June 9, 1878.)

SCRIPTURE : Prov. iv.   HYMNS : 560, 632, 684.

THE ROCK OF OUR REFUGE.

—o—

In the shadow of the Rock let me rest,
When I feel the tempest's shock thrill my breast ;
All in vain the storm shall sweep while I hide,
And my tranquil station keep by Thy side.

On the parch'd and desert way where I tread,
With the scorching noon-tide ray o'er my head,
Let me find the welcome shade, cool and still,
And my weary steps be stayed while I will.

I in peace will rest me there, till I see
That the skies again are fair over me—
That the burning heats are past, and the day
Bids the traveller at last go his way.

Then my pilgrim staff I'll take, and once more
I'll my onward journey make as before ;
And with joyous heart and strong I will raise
Unto Thee, O Rock, a song glad with praise !

RAY PALMER.

XII.

TRUST AND PRAY.

"For the people shall dwell in Zion at Jerusalem : thou shalt weep no more : he will be very gracious unto thee at the voice of thy cry ; when he shall hear it, he will answer thee."—*Isa.* xxx. 19.

———

O LORD God, the strength and the hope of Thy people, we would approach Thee through Jesus Christ Thy Son with notes of thanksgiving, for we are not ashamed of our hope, neither has our confidence led us into confusion. We have proven it to be true, that they that trust in the Lord shall be as mount Zion, which can never be moved, which abideth for ever. We trusted in Thee with regard to our innumerable sins, and Thou hast cast them behind Thy back. We trusted in Thee, yea, we trusted in Thee when many evils compassed us about, and we were sore beset with temptation and Thou broughtest us out into a wealthy place : Thou didst set our feet upon a rock and establish our goings. We trusted in Thee, alas ! too feebly, in the hour of our distress when we were troubled exceedingly with earthly things, still Thou didst not fail us though our faith trembled : though we believed not Thou didst abide faithful. The Lord hath helped His people, yea the Lord hath been the strength and the help of His chosen. "Many are the afflictions of the righteous, but the Lord delivereth him out of them all," and at this moment, in looking back upon the past, we have nothing to do but to admire and to adore the constancy of love, the faithfulness of grace.

We thank Thee, O God, on the behalf of many of Thy people, our brethren, that Thou hast dealt so well with them. We knew them many years ago when their young hearts first believed in Thee, and here they are still the living, the living in Zion, to praise Thee as they do this day. Their feet have sometimes almost gone, their steps have well nigh slipped, but Thou hast held them up, and they are walking in their integrity, preserved as only grace could preserve them, living still to praise Thy name. We bless Thee on the behalf of the much tried among Thy children. They went through fire and through water; men did go over their heads, yet hast Thou preserved them. Their hope seemed to wither like the fading leaf, and the summer of their joy turned into a bleak winter of adversity, yet hath the spring time come to them and the time of the singing of birds, yea, they begin to pluck their first ripe fruits, and they joy and exult in the Lord.

O Lord, we praise Thee for keeping alive a testimony for the truth in the land. There have been dark and evil days, and some that professed to be Thy servants have turned traitors to the gospel; yet still Thou hast heard the cry of the faithful, and the candle is not put out, neither hath the sun gone down, but even unto this day the Lord, the God of Israel reigneth in the midst of His people and His saints exult in His name.

And now with this thankfulness upon our hearts, we would humbly ask Thee to strengthen us as to our future confidence in Thee. Are there any of Thy servants here at this time, or anywhere all over the world, whose confidence begins to fail them by reason of present affliction or deep depression of spirit? We beseech Thee strengthen the things that remain that are ready to die, and let their faith no longer waver, but may they become strong in the Lord in full assurance of faith. Oh God, thou knowest the burden of every heart before Thee, the secret sighing of the prisoner cometh up into Thine ears. Some of us are in perplexity, others are in actual suffering of body. Some are sorely cast down in themselves, and others deeply afflicted with the trials of those they love, but as for all these burdens our soul would cast them on the Lord—in quietness and confidence shall be our strength, and we would this morning, all without exception who are tried and troubled, take up the place of sitting still, leaving with quiet acquiescence everything in the hands of God. Great Helmsman, Thou shalt steer the ship and we will not be troubled. By Thy grace we will leave everything most sweetly in Thy hands. Where else should these things be left? and we will take up the note of joyous song in anticipation of the deliverance which will surely come.

Save Thy people from unbelief, save them from confidence in the creature. Bring us one and all to be as to the world even as a weaned child. May we have done with these things, and as to Thee, O Lord, may we with strong desire seek after yet more of Thee, and cling to Thee as our sure confidence for evermore.

As for the future, we desire to bless Thy name that Thou hast covered it from our eyes, nor would we wish to lift even a corner of the veil which hides from us the things that are to be, but we delight to feel that He who hast ruled all things for our good changeth not. It may be Thou hast appointed for us great torrents of tribulation, but Thou wilt be with us if we pass through the river. Perhaps Thou wilt permit us to go through blazing fires of persecution or temptation, but we shall not be burned, for Thou hast assured us it shall be so, that we shall go through the fires unhurt since Thou wilt be with us.

Peradventure it is written in the tablets of Thine eternal purpose that we shall soon end this mortal life and die. Well, be it so, we shall the sooner see Thy face, the sooner drink eternal draughts of bliss. But if Thou hast appointed for us grey hairs and a long and weary time of the taking down of the tabernacle, only grant us grace that by infirmity our faith may never fail us, but when the windows are darkened may we still look out to see the hope that is to be revealed; and when the grasshopper becometh a burden still let our strength be as our days, even to the last day.

We now commit ourselves again to Thy keeping, O faithful Creator; to Thy keeping, O Saviour of the pierced hand; to Thy keeping, O eternal Spirit, Thou who art able to keep us from falling, and sanctify us fully that we may be made to stand among the saints in light. O God, we can trust Thee, and we do. Our faith has gathered strength by the lapse of years. Each following birthday, we trust, confirms us in the fact that to rely upon God is our happiness and our strength, and we will do so, though the earth be removed and the mountains be carried into the midst of the sea. We will not fear since God abideth fast for ever, and His covenant cannot fail.

And now to-day wilt thou lead others to trust Thee. Oh be Thou so revealed wherever the congregations are met together, that men may come to Thee and live. Oh that the people in this house this morning, might not one of them go away unbelievers. If they have been indifferent to these things and have never studied the ground of the believer's confidence, may they see it clearly this morning, and accept of it as the rock on which they shall build. Oh if there be in this audience, as we fear there must be, many that are living to trust in their wealth, or their talents, or their position in life, or who are trusting in nothing but raising their building without a foundation at all, Oh bring them this day to see that there is nothing worthy of an immortal soul's confidence except the immortal and everliving God, and this day come by Christ Jesus unto the Father. May many a heart end all its weary wanderings and sit still at Christ's feet and see the salvation of God.

God bless our country ! May faith be multiplied in the land ! Preserve our nation at this juncture. Guide, we pray Thee, the deliberations of councillors and princes. May peace be preserved, and at the same time may the great purposes of God with regard to the spread of liberty and of the gospel be subserved by every decree of the council. O God, we beseech Thee, ease the world of the sway of every evil principle. Let the day come when all classes of men shall study the interest of others as well as their own, when the various nations shall yield to the one sceptre of Christ and like kindred tribes shall melt into one. Yea, hasten His coming and His reign when the shout shall go up to heaven that the " Lord God omnipotent reigneth."

As Thou bidst us, we pray for all in authority over us, especially asking that every blessing may rest upon the Queen. We pray for other nations also, and especially for countries and colonies where our language is spoken and our God is worshipped—may the Lord's choicest blessings rest there. We also put up special prayer for any of our dear friends that are in trouble, asking Thee to help some who have been suffering bitter bereavement, others who are vexed with sickness in their own persons. The Lord be pleased to be gracious unto all who trust Him, and to make them trust Him in the darkest hour. And now, unto the Father, the Son, and to the Holy Ghost, Israel's one God, be glory throughout all the world. Amen and Amen.

SERMON : No. 1419. (June 16, 1878.)

SCRIPTURE : Isaiah xxx. HYMNS : 125, 747.

XIII.

KING AND PRIEST.

" Even he shall build the temple of the Lord ; and he shall bear
the glory, and shall sit and rule upon his throne ; and he shall be a
priest upon his throne ; and the counsel of peace shall be between
them both."—*Zech.* vi. 13.

———

GLORIOUS God, it is the flower of our being to
worship Thee. this is the crown and glory of life,
to adore and worship the Life-giver from whom all good
things come. Worship hath often been to us as a bath in
heavenly pleasure, and we have come out of it refreshed
and comforted, blessed, and filled with heavenly delight.
Oh for the Holy Spirit's power to help us in worship now !
Breathe upon us, Oh Divine Spirit, and let that breath
cause us to forget the world, but bring us into the fullest
life in the contemplation of God and heaven.

Blessed God, Father, Son, and Spirit, our whole
spirit would reverence Thee, yet would we have such
knowledge of Thy goodness that we might not be over-
awed with Thy greatness; such a sense of Thy nearness
in the person of Jesus Christ. the Man, the Branch,
that we might not be driven away with terror, but

may be drawn near with filial love and holy boldness. Lord, there was once a great gulf between us, but Thou hast bridged that gulf, for now the Lord Jesus Christ is brother to our souls, yet is He Son of the Highest; truly man, yet truly God, He is the Interpreter, one of a thousand, the Daysman, who doth this day lay His hand upon us both. Oh how we joy in Christ, and Thou dost joy in Him too. We long to glorify Him, and Thou dost delight to glorify Thy Son. We would set Him on high, and Thou hast set Him "far above all principalities and powers, and every name that is named."

Now this day we pray Thee, " behold our Shield and look upon the face of Thine Anointed ; " and while we shelter behind Him as a shield, let Him stand for us, and let the glory of God in the face of Jesus Christ be seen, that Thou mayest be precious to us unworthy ones.

But, O Lord, we worship with all our heart and adore the Father, the Son, and the Holy Ghost ; and Oh most blessed Lamb of God, with all the saints before the throne, we pay Thee reverence—casting all that we have before Thee. Crowns we have none, not even of silver and gold, but such as Thou hast graciously given, we would willingly lay at Thy feet, content to feel that everything is ours when it is Thine, and the more ours when we have yielded it up to Thee. We wish we could live for Jesus wholly, that there were no distractions, no secondary channels into which the stream of life could flow, but that as He is all to us, so all of us might be unto Him alone.

And now we present ourselves before the Throne of God, in the name of Jesus Christ our great High Priest. And first, we ask for pardon through the blessed blood.

Some of us Thou hast already pardoned: give us a new sense of it. Continue to pardon us; let us feel as if we came every day to the "fountain filled with blood," and as if the washing were every day new. But, oh, have pity upon some that have never been pardoned. Hear the cry of sinners as they seek Thy face, and wherever there is a penitent spirit be pleased speedily to send it relief, and let forgiveness of sin be felt wherever the burden of sin weighs down the spirit.

Next would we ask Thee to subdue our iniquities. Lord, conquer the power of sin in all of us. Grant us power to live above it; let not the passions of the flesh, nor the lustings of the mind, bring the spirit into subjection; but may our spirit rule over mind and body; and may Christ rule over our spirit, and so may we know the "liberty wherewith Christ makes us free."

Next we ask for perfect consecration, that everything we are and have may be the Lord's, not in name, but in deed and in truth.

And then we ask for fruitfulness. Oh, help us to bring forth the fruits of the Spirit to the glory of God. May our character get more beautiful every day. If there are any traces of Christ's artistic work upon us, may He go on with that Divine pencil until He shall have produced in us a perfect character, and we shall be among men copies of the perfectness of our Master.

O Lord, we do ask Thee to make us fit for heaven. We hope it is not long before we shall be there. We have sometimes had glimpses between the gates of pearl; we have had such foretastes of the "place prepared," that sometimes we are in haste to be gone; the flavour of the grapes of Eschol is in our mouths, and we long to be where all the clusters grow. But we are conscious of unfitness for that state as yet. Oh, go on, most blessed Spirit, with Thy patient work, until Thou shalt have made us heavenly, and then we shall be caught up to the "heavenly places," to see the face of our Beloved.

Yet let not all Thy saints be gone as yet. Spare us some, we pray Thee, to build up Thy church below; for that they should abide with us is expedient for our weakness—that they may help us, that they may be to us instead of eyes, for they know where to encamp in the wilderness. Thou hast taught them experimentally Thy word, and filled them with an unction from the Holy One, and, therefore, for our sakes let not Thy saints be hastened home for a while. We breathe this prayer with bated breath, because there is One who prays against us, whose prayer must always have the first reply; it is even He, the Well Beloved, whom our ears can hear saying at this moment: "Father, I will that they whom Thou hast given Me be with Me where I am." O Lord Jesus, take us whensoever Thou wilt!

Now, standing thus before the throne of God without fear, we would humbly ask Thee to bless our country. Oh that Thou wouldst look upon this nation which has sorely sinned, which has turned away from the path of peace to seek the ways of glory and of blood. O Lord, be pleased to turn its course aright again. We beseech Thee bring us out of the disasters which we have been made to suffer, and let the nation lie penitent at the feet of God. Oh that the Christian party in this realm might prevail—that the Church of God might have a little influence over the worldly mass. Oh that the time were come when the salt shall more completely savour all the masses, and the glorious leaven shall work until all the measures of meal are leavened.

We do ask Thee Lord to give power to truth, to righteousness, to godliness, to peace, and to every other principle which is favoured of the Lord of heaven; and let this land be delivered from the curse of the Papacy, from all the incoming both of rationalism and ritualism; and let the truth as it is in Jesus prevail, not only here but everywhere, till the whole " earth is filled with the knowledge of the glory of God as the waters cover the sea."

Bless other nations also, we pray Thee, and the church of God in every land. For the saints of every tongue we pray, especially for those of our own kith and kin, scattered across the ocean hither and thither.

Make the whole of Thy people to be full of life and vigour, and may the day come when the missionary spirit shall be more fully caught by the church at home, and they that have gone forth shall bring tens of thousands to be built into the temple of God.

O Lord we wait upon Thee now, and ask the over-shadowing of Thy presence ! Jesus of Nazareth, pass by

just now ! Divine Spirit, rest upon us now ! Holy
Father, look upon Thy children now, and make this place
to be glorious at this good hour !   We ask it in the name
of the Well Beloved.   Amen.

SERMON : No. 1495.   (September 21, 1879.)

SCRIPTURE : Ps. cx.   Zech. vi. 9-15.   Eph. ii. 11-22.

HYMNS : 154, 419, 395.

XIV.

THE SIN OF MISTRUST OF GOD.

"And the Lord said unto Moses, How long will this people provoke Me? and how long will it be ere they believe Me, for all the signs which I have shewed among them?"—*Num.* xiv. 11.

———

OUR Father, blessed be the grace and love which have taught us to use that dear familiar name—"Our Father, which art in heaven," and therefore highest and most exalted, and worthy to be breathed with awe and reverence by all that draw near to Thee.

"Hallowed be Thy Name." Oh that all the earth would ever reverence it. As for ourselves, enable us by Thy grace to use it with awe and trembling; and may a consideration of the glorious character which is intended by Thy gracious name, ever lay us in the very dust before Thee, and yet lift us up with holy joy and with an unwavering confidence. We come before Thee this morning through Christ Jesus to express our entire confidence in Thee. We believe that Thou art, and that Thou art the rewarder of them that diligently seek Thee.

Glorious Jehovah, the God of Abraham, of Isaac, and of Jacob, Thou hast not changed: Thou art still a covenant God, and Thou keepest that covenant to all Thy people ; neither dost Thou permit a single word of it to fall to the ground. All Thy promises are yea and amen in Christ Jesus to Thy glory by us, and we believe those promises will be fulfilled in every jot and title : not one of them shall want its mate, not one of them shall fall to the ground like the frivolous words of men. Hast Thou said and wilt Thou not do it? Hast Thou commanded and shall it not come to pass? We are utterly ashamed and full of confusion, because we have to confess that we have doubted Thee. Many of our actions have been atheistic. We have lived at times as if there were no God.

Lord, forgive us that death in life, in which so many of our years were spent, when we found something in the world apart from Thee, and were content with the things of the hour, the vile shadows, transient gusts of things which truly are not, for Thou alone art all in all. We have repented, as Thou knowest, through Thy grace, most bitterly of that time of death in which we tried to live ; and now Thou hast given us to see our pardon in the wounds of Jesus, and our soul doth put her trust in Him. God incarnate is the ground of our hope that we are accepted and forgiven, notwithstanding that previous life of ours.

But Lord, the worst of it is, that in many of our actions, even since then, we betray a disbelief of Thee. Like the children of Israel in the wilderness, Thou mayest well say of us, "How long will it be ere they believe Me, though I have shewn all my signs and wonders among them?" O God Thou hast been very faithful to Thy servants till now. In no one instance is there a breach of promise. Thou hast tried us as silver is tried, but in very faithfulness Thou hast afflicted us. Thou hast brought us very low indeed, but underneath us have still been the everlasting arms. Thou hast brought us into the wilderness, but Thou hast furnished a table for us in the presence of our enemies.

Thou hast made us to see the end of all perfection, but Thy love, even then, has been perfected—perfected in our weakness. Thou art all goodness, and truth, and grace, and loving kindness; and therefore blessed be Thy name for ever and ever.

And now blot out the sin of Thy servants. Once again let this unbelief of ours be forgiven, and let us stand, with no sin upon the conscience, but absolved through Jesu's blood, in the enjoyment of such confidence with Thee, that we may lift up our face without a cloud, and may trust in Thee henceforth without a doubt, and go on our way rejoicing whatever that way may be.

Lord teach us to be resigned to Thy will; teach us to delight in Thy law; teach us to have no will but Thy will; teach us to be sure that everything Thou doest is good—is the very best that can be done. Help us to leave our concerns in Thy divine hands, being persuaded that Thou hast sway even over evil; that out of it Thou bringest good, and better still, and better still in infinite progression, till Thy high purposes shall develop in Thine own perfect glory, and in the perfect bliss of all them that put their trust in Thee.

Are any of Thy servants this morning in great trial? Lord help them. Whatever they fail in, let them not fail in faith. May we scorn to doubt our God. Oh let not the devil get so much power over us as to cause us to mistrust the Eternal, who must not be mistrusted, but may we glorify Thee. May we snatch the great opportunities of glorifying Thee which troubles and trials bring, and count ourselves to have a high talent committed to us when we have the opportunity of showing our conquest of self and our glorying in God in the time of trial. The Lord bless His people here with Abrahamic faith, which staggers not at the promise through unbelief.

O God, have mercy upon the unbelievers that are here this morning, who have heard Thy word, and who profess to believe in the inspiration of Thy sacred Book, and yet have never come and put their confidence in Christ. We know that they are condemned already, because they have not believed upon the Son of God. But oh deliver them from this great sin, and may they come at this very hour, and cast their helpless souls upon Him on Whom Thou hast laid our help. May they begin to believe this morning, and then they shall begin to live ; and Thou wilt breathe peace into such, and Thou wilt give them rest, and strength, and holiness, and they shall be more than conquerors if they will but believe their God.

O Lord, we beseech Thee, save our unconverted friends and neighbours from this gall of bitterness, this horrible yoke of iniquity which consists in disbelieving God and His Christ.

And, then, deliver any of Thy children that have back-slidden, and have got into a state of misbelief. May they be brought back ; may they come with weeping and lamentation, and again trust the ever-blessed Father ; and may our confidence become strong that our peace may be like a river, and our righteousness like the waves of the sea.

God bless this beloved church ! Give to it more faith : may the prayers that go up before Thee be salted with faith : when we preach, may we preach in faith, and may all that is done of the brotherhood for Christ, be done in simple confidence in God. We know that if we believe not we shall never be established. We cannot expect to see result from our service except it is done in faith ; for Thou hast said " According to thy faith be it unto thee." O give the thousands of members of this church the childlike simplicity that never thinks of doubting God, but may we go forward—in all weakness made strong by the strength of the Mighty God of Jacob.

Give a blessing this morning, we pray Thee, to us all ; may we make a distinct advance in the divine life ; may we get to a higher platform ; may we leave the mists of doubt and fear below us in the valley, and quit the marshes of the plain, and climb the glittering hill-tops of eternal security in Christ and blessed oneness with Him, by simply believing Him who cannot lie—who hath sworn by two immutable things and cannot from His purpose turn, nor from His word draw back. O God, grant this faith to the entire church.

We believe the world will be brought in, when the church believes her God : the Kingdom will come, and the glory shall be made visible to all flesh, when once we have the confidence we ought to have in Him who is worthy to be praised, and to be trusted evermore. And now by the precious blood of Jesus accept this feeble prayer of ours, and send down a shower of benedictions ; and to the Father, to the Son, and to the Holy Ghost, be glory for ever and ever. Amen.

SERMON : No. 1498. (October 5, 1879.)

SCRIPTURE: Num. xiii. 20-23, xiv. 1-25, Heb. iii. 7-19.

HYMNS : 192, 239, 670.

XV.

THE FOOT-WASHING.

"Jesus knowing that the Father had given all things unto his hands, and that he was come from God, and went to God; He riseth from supper, and laid aside his garments; and took a towel, and girded himself. After that he poureth water into a bason, and began to wash the disciples' feet, and to wipe them with the towel wherewith he was girded."—*John* xiii. 3-5.

———

O JEHOVAH, our God, Thou lovest Thy people, Thou hast placed all the saints in the hand of Jesus, and Thou hast given Jesus to be to them a Leader, a Commander, and a Husband; and we know that Thou delightest to hear us cry on the behalf of Thy church, for Thou carest for Him, and Thou art ready to grant to Him according to the covenant provisions which Thou hast laid up in store for Christ Jesus. Therefore would we begin this morning's prayer, by entreating Thee to behold and visit the vine, and the vineyard which Thy right hand hath planted. Look upon Zion the city of our solemnities, look upon those whom Thou hast chosen from before the foundation of the world, whom Christ hath redeemed with blood, whose hearts He has won and holds, and who are His own though they be in the world.

Holy Father, keep Thy people we beseech Thee, for Jesus' sake: though they are in the world let them not be of it; but may there be a marked distinction between them and the rest of mankind. Even as their Lord was " holy, harmless, undefiled, and separate from sinners," so may it be with believers in Christ. May they follow Him; and may they not know the voice of strangers, but come out from the rest, that they may follow Him without the camp.

We cry to Thee this morning for the preservation of Thy church in the world, and especially for her purity. Oh Father, keep us, we beseech Thee, with all keeping, that the Evil one touch us not. We shall be tempted, but let him not prevail against us. In a thousand ways he will lay snares for our feet, but, oh, deliver us as a bird from the snare of the fowler. May the snare be broken that we may escape.

Let not the church suffer dishonour at any time, but may her garments be always white. Let not such as come in among her, that are not of her, utterly despoil her. Oh Christ, as Thou didst groan concerning Judas, so may Thy children cry to Thee concerning any that have fallen aside into crooked ways, lest the cause of Christ in the earth should be dishonoured. Oh God, cover we beseech Thee, with Thy feathers, all the people of Christ, and keep Thy church even until He shall come who, having loved His own that were in the world, loveth them even to the end.

We would each one of us ask this morning that we may be washed as to our feet : we trust Thou hast bathed us once for all in the sin-removing fountain. Thou hast also washed us in the waters of regeneration, and given us the renewing of our minds through Jesus Christ. But oh for daily cleansing ! Dost Thou see any fault in us ?—oh we know that Thou dost—wash us that we may be clean. Are we deficient in any virtue ? Oh supply it, that we may exhibit a perfect character, to the glory of Him who hast made us anew in Christ Jesus. Or, is there something that would be good, carried to excess ? Be pleased to modify it lest one virtue should slaughter another, and we should not be the image of Christ completely. Oh Lord and Master, Thou who didst wash Thy disciples' feet of old, still be very patient toward us, very condescending towards our provoking faults, and go on with us, we pray Thee, till Thy great work shall be completed, and we shall be brethren of the First-born, like unto Him.

Gracious Master, we wish to conquer self in every respect; we desire to live for the glory of God and the good of our fellow men. We would have it true of us as of our Master, " He saved others, Himself He cannot save." Wilt Thou enable us especially to overcome the body with all its affections and lusts ; may the flesh be kept under; let no appetite of any kind, of the grosser sort, prevail against our manhood, lest we be dishonoured and unclean. And let not even the most refined power of the natural mind be permitted to come so .forward as to mar the dominion of the Spirit of God within us.

Oh help us not to be so easily moved, even by pain : may we have much patience ; and let not the prospect of death ever cause us any fear, but may the Spirit get the mastery of the body. We know nothing can hurt the true man—the inner, new born, cannot be smitten ; nor is it to die : it is wholly incorruptible, and liveth and abideth for ever in the life that is in Christ Jesus.

Oh for a complete conquest of self : especially render us insensible to praise, lest we be too sensitive to censure. Let us reckon that to have the approbation of God, and of our own conscience, is quite enough ; and may we be content, gracious God, to hear the cavillings of unreasonable men ; yea, and to hear the misrepresentations of our own brethren. Those that we love, if they love not us, yet may we love them none the less ; and if by mistake they misjudge us, let us have no hard feelings towards them : and God grant we may never misjudge one another. Doth not our Judge stand at the door ?

Oh keep us like little children who do not know, but expect to know hereafter, and are content to believe things which they do not understand. Lord keep us humble, dependent, yet serenely joyful. May we be calm and quiet even as a weaned child, yet may we be earnest and active.

Oh Saviour, make us like Thyself; we wish not so much to do, as to be. If Thou wilt make us to be right, we shall do right. We have often to put a constraint upon ourselves to be right ; but oh, that we were like Thee, Jesus, so that we had but to act out ourselves to act out perfect holiness. We shall never rest till this is the case, till Thou hast made us to be inwardly holy; and then words and actions must be holy as a matter of course.

Now here we are, Lord, and we belong to Thee. We caught at that word as we read it—"Having loved His own." Oh, it is because we are Thine own, that we have hope. Thou wilt make us worthy of Thee. Thy possession of us is our hope of perfection. Thou dost wash our feet because we are Thine own. Oh how sweet is the mercy which first took us to its heart, and made us all its own, and now continues to deal tenderly with us that, being Christ's own, we may have that of Christ within us which all may see and which proves us to be the Lord's.

Now this morning, we would bring before Thee all Thy saints, and ask Thee to attend to their trials and troubles. Some we know here are afflicted in person, others are afflicted in their dear friends; some are afflicted in their temporal estate, and are brought into sore distress. Lord, we do not know the trials of all Thy people, but Thou dost; for Thou art the Head, and the pains of all the members are centred in Thee. Help all Thy people even to the end.

Now we pray Thee to grant us the Sabbath blessing which we have already sought; and let it come upon all the churches of our beloved country. May the Lord revive true and undefiled religion here, and in all the other lands where Christ is known and preached: and let the day come when heathendom shall become converted, when the crescent of Mohammed shall wane into eternal night, and when she that sitteth on the Seven Hills, and exalteth herself in the place of God, shall be cast down

to sink like a millstone in the flood. Let the blessed
gospel of the Eternal God prevail : let the whole earth
be filled with His glory. Oh that we may live to see that
day !

The Lord bless our country : have pity upon it in all
its present afflicted condition. God bless Her Majesty
the Queen with every mercy and blessing. Grant that
there may be, in Thine infinite wisdom, a change in the
state of trade and commerce, that there may be no complaint and distress. Oh, let the people see Thy hand,
and understand why it is laid upon them, that they may
turn from wrong-doing, and seek righteousness and follow
peace. The Lord hear us as, in secret, we often cry to
Thee on behalf of our beloved land : the Lord lift up the
light of His countenance upon it yet again, for Jesus' sake.
Amen.

SERMON : No. 1499.   (October 12, 1879.)

SCRIPTURE : John xiii. 1-17.   HYMNS : 186, 262, 263.

XVI.

THE LIFE LOOK!

" And as Moses lifted up the serpent in the wilderness, even so must the Son of Man be lifted up ; That whosoever believeth in Him should not perish, but have eternal life."—*John* iii. 14, 15.

OUR Father, we wish this morning to come to Thee anew in Christ Jesus. Many of us can look back to the happy moment when first we saw the law fulfilled in Christ, wrath appeased, death destroyed, sin forgiven, and our souls saved. Oh it was a happy morning—a blessed time. Never did the sun seem to shine so brightly as then, when we beheld the Sun of Righteousness, and basked in His light. Many days have passed since then with some of us, and every day we have had proofs of the faithfulness of God to the gospel of His Son. We have proved the power of Jesus' blood for daily cleansing ; we have proved the power of His Divine Spirit for daily teaching, guidance, and sanctification ; and now we want no other rock to build upon than that which we have built upon ; we desire no other hope, nor even to dream of any other, but that hope which Thou hast set before us in the Gospel, to which hope we have fled for refuge, and which hope we still have as an anchor of the soul, both sure and steadfast.

But Lord, we would still begin again this morning by looking unto Jesus Christ anew—whatever may be our sin, whatever Thy pure and holy eye can see amiss in us, which we cannot see: we desire to come to Jesus as sinners, guilty, lost, ruined by nature, and again to give the faith look, and to behold Him hanging on the cross for us.

Thou knowest with what heartiness, and depths of truthfulness, we can say, " Lord, I believe, help Thou mine unbelief." We again declare that all our hope is centred in the atoning Sacrifice, and in the risen Saviour, who has gone into the glory as the testimony of our justification, and of our acceptance in Him. Oh dear Saviour, if in the course of years we have tried to add anything to the one foundation, if unconsciously we are relying now upon our knowledge, our experience, our Christian effort, we desire to clear away all this heap of rags and get down on the foundation again. None but Jesus! None but Jesus! Our soul rests in none but Jesus ; and we hate and loathe, with our inmost nature, the very idea of adding anything to what He has finished, or attempting to complete what is perfect in Him.

Oh this morning let Thy people feel that there is now no condemnation to them. Let them feel the completeness of the washing Christ has given, the blessed fulness of the righteousness which Christ has imputed, the eternal vitality of that life with which Christ has endowed us, the indissoluble character of that union by which we are knit to Christ by ties that never can be broken ; and may we to-day rejoice in Christ Jesus, and have no confidence in the flesh ; and do Thou write upon our hearts these blessed words, "Filled with all the fulness of God," and may we know it is so, that we have all that we can hold ; and may we be praying to be enlarged, that we may take in even more of Christ than we have as yet received ; for He is all ours, altogether ours, and ours world without end.

And now, Lord, we beseech Thee to help all in this house to look to Jesus Christ alone. Peradventure some backsliders here are questioning whether they ever did believe in Jesus. May they leave that question alone and believe in Him now. May they be content to let the past go by the wall, and once for all come, if they never did come, and embrace the Saviour whom Thou, great God, hast set forth as all-sufficient to save. Let Peter weep bitterly, but let him come to his Master again. Oh, let the most wandering cry to Thee, and may they look to Thy holy temple ; and as they look, let the eternal life stream into them again, by the energy of the Eternal Spirit; and may they feel that whatever may have been the past, they are restored like prodigal children to a feast of love, restored for ever to the Father's house.

There may be some here that are so tossed about mentally, that are so dismayed with inward temptation, so out of their wits by the assaults of Satan, that they know not what to do. Lord when they have no wit, give them wit enough to trust Christ ; and when they can do nothing else, may they faint away upon the bosom of Eternal Love. The Lord help His servants, when they are in extremity, to feel that now is the time for God to begin; and when they are driven over the very verge of hope, and the precipice of despair is before them, oh grant them grace to fall into the arms of Jesus, and there shall they find life from the dead.

But oh look in great mercy upon the many that may be here, who never have believed in Jesus. O Strong Son of God, Immortal Love, whom, though we have not seen Thy face, we do believe in, and rely upon, ride forth this morning with Thine arrows dipped in Thine own blood, and shoot them out amongst this audience, that the people may fall under them, wounded with the sense of sin, smitten even to self-despair with a consciousness of guilt: and oh that they might get healing from the hands that wound them, may they get life from the hand that kills their hope. May they look to Thee, anointed of the Lord, ennobled in the highest heaven, who once received the sinner here below in Thine own Person, and who still receiveth sinners: oh that they might come to Thee and live. There are many that are now joining us, great God, in this prayer, that we may have many conversions this very morning. We mean to look, and wait, and watch for it. We ask that this very morning, while Jesus Christ is lifted up, many may look unto Him and be cured of the serpent's bite for ever. Thou hast promised to hear Thy people's prayer, and this is a prayer that must be according to Thy mind ; and it is for the honour of Thy dear Son ; and it is put up in faith, put up in faith in Jesus; therefore Thou canst not run back from it, but Thou must keep that word to which in humble, but adoring faith, we hold Thee—" My word shall not return unto me void." Give us then a great increase to the church by the preaching of the gospel this morning.

The like blessing we ask for all churches, and for all ministers of the gospel of Jesus. We ask for a revival of true godliness all over the world. We pray Thee to grant that these disastrous times may drive Thy children nearer to Thee ; may deliver many of them from a worldly spirit ; and may it come to pass that while they grow poor one way they may grow rich in another, by the sanctification of their losses and afflictions.

God be gracious to this land. Send us, we pray Thee, the Holy Spirit more abundantly than ever ; and may there be myriads born to Christ in these latter days. So do Thou with all the nations, till all lands shall bow before Thee, and all generations shall call Thee blessed.

We offer special prayers this morning for the rising generation. The Lord bless our Sabbath Schools. Teach the teachers, bless and superintend the superintendents, and let the schools be more than ever a place where the lambs are cared for and tended, that they may grow up as sheep of the fold of Jesus. Many prayers have been offered already to-day for this end : we pray Thee hear them all, and let the richest benisons of heaven rest on those devoted men and women, who deny themselves many privileges that they may have the greater privilege of feeding the lambs of Christ. The Lord hear us and do for us exceeding abundantly above what we ask or even think, through Jesus Christ our Lord. Amen.

SERMON : No. 1500. (October 19, 1879.)

SCRIPTURE : Num. xxi. 4-9. John iii. 1-18.

HYMNS : 240, 539, 331.

ALONE WITH THEE.

—o—

ALONE with Thee, alone with Thee.
   Now through my breast
There steals a breath, like breath of balm,
That healing brings, and holy calm,
That soothes like chanted song or psalm,
   And makes me blest.

Alone with Thee, alone with Thee,
   In Thy pure light
The splendid pomps and shows of time,
The tempting steeps that pride would climb,
The peaks where glory rests sublime,
   Pale on my sight.

Alone with Thee, alone with Thee,
   My softened heart
Floats on the flood of love divine,
Feels all its wishes drowned in Thine;
Content that every good is mine
   Thou canst impart.

Alone with Thee, alone with Thee,
   I want no more
To make my earthly bliss complete,
Than oft my Lord unseen to meet:
For " sight " I wait till tread my feet
   Yon glistening shore.

RAY PALMER.

XVII.

REFUGES OF LIES.

"Judgment also will I lay to the line, and righteousness to the plummet: and the hail shall sweep away the refuge of lies, and the waters shall overflow the hiding-place."—*Isa.* xxviii. 17.

———

O LORD, how shall we speak with thee, for we are dust and ashes! May Thy Spirit speak in us, that we may speak unto Thy Spirit. And how shall we draw near to Thee, for we have no merits. Let the merits of Jesus stand for us, that we may acceptably approach our God, being "accepted in the Beloved." Lord, we are full of infirmities, and full of wants, and full of sin, and we come and cast ourselves at Thy feet. Being nothing, we would ask to receive everything of Thee ; and being altogether undeserving, we would look to Thy loving kindness and tender mercy, and expect much from that divine source, through Jesus Christ Thy Son.

Help Thy servant now to pray for all this people, and may there be a voice in our prayer for every man's want before Thee. At the same time, help all this company to be instant in prayer ; and may there not be a prayerless heart in the whole building, but may every man, and every woman too, come with his own request and burden, and may it be done unto him according to Thy grace.

First we would lie humbly before Thee, confessing our sin, our frequent sin, our wilful sin; our sin against light and knowledge; sins of heart and thought, sins of word and sins of action. There is no power of body, or of the will, which has not been defiled with sin; and we confess this before Thee with much shame. So great has been the stream, that we are sure there must be a deep and large fount of pollution within our nature, and Thou hast made some of us to know that it is so. Thou hast taken us into the chambers of imagery, that are within our spirit, and we have dug through the wall, and have gone from one chamber to another; and the deeper we search, the more we are shocked, and the further we have pryed into the secrets of our being, the more are we utterly ashamed that we should be such creatures as we are by nature.

We have been saying to Thee this morning, as we marked the leaves falling from the trees, "We are altogether as an unclean thing, and all our righteousnesses are as filthy rags." "We all do fade as a leaf, and our iniquities, like the wind, have taken us away." As the wind strips the leaves from the trees and leaves them bare, so we stand before Thee this morning. We have not by nature one green shoot or anything like fruit: we are unprofitable altogether, and only fit to be "hewn down and cast into the fire": for what fruit we have borne, if it has been the fruit of our nature, has been more the fruit of thorns and thistles, than of figs and grapes.

Lord God, we wonder Thou didst ever have any
mercy on us at all ; for in justice and judgment, if we
were set upon the Throne, we could do no other than
condemn ourselves, for there is no plea against Thy
justice that can be found within our lives or nature.

Yet, Lord, we thank Thee that Thou hast saved
many of us, and we would this morning exult in that
salvation, and pray that all the rest here assembled might
be saved also !

O God, Thou hast smitten a heavy blow at our proud
self ; Thou hast made us lie broken in pieces before
Thee.   Thou hast set up another in the place of the false
god that ruled us.   We do not live for self, nor even for
self-salvation.   Jesus Christ has become the Lord and
Master of our spirit, and He has delivered us from the
dominion of self and sin, and helped us to be obedient
unto Thee.   Now, henceforth, the strongest portion of
our will is towards holiness.   Oh, that we could be
perfectly holy ! we sigh after it and cry after it: we think
we could bear all trials, we feel persuaded we could give
up all pleasures, if we might but win the pleasure of
complete obedience to God.   This, indeed, is the target
towards which, like arrows shot from an archer's bow, our
lives are speeding.   Though rough winds turn us aside,
yet shall we strike the target by Thy grace.

The Lord be pleased to help us every day to put
down sin.   O Lord, whenever pride arises, may we be
more than ever humbled in Thy sight.   Whenever self
comes up, may we be determined it shall not live,
but flee to the precious blood, that we may slay it.   Lord,

save us from self; save us from the love of the world;
save us from the pride of the eye, and the pride of life;
save us, we beseech Thee, from everything that is natural
to fallen man, and let the new nature which Thou hast
planted manifest itself day by day, till we shall be made
like unto Christ, "whom having not seen we love," but
to whom we shall be conformed, for we shall "see Him
as He is."

Look with great grace, we pray Thee, O Lord, upon
the slaves of sin that are present here this morning:
break their fetters. Oh, save this people. We know
there are some in this house that as yet are in the "gall
of bitterness, and in the bond of iniquity." Move, O
Divine Spirit, over this audience, and fetch out from
among us those that know not God, that they may know
themselves and their God this day. Oh make this to be
a profitable, soul-winning Sabbath, one of the high days
on which heaven's bells shall ring out more sweetly than
ever, because many and many a prodigal child has come
back to the Father's house to make the Father glad.

Save souls, we pray Thee, all over the world. Where-
ever Jesus Christ is lifted up, may He "draw all men
to Him," and may a great multitude look to Him and
be lightened, that their faces may no more be ashamed!

And now, Lord, look upon this people for good.
Thou knowest the troubles of every burdened spirit.
Thou knowest how some whom Thou lovest are sick;
how others have to watch over their dearest ones fading
away and withering like flowers. Lord, send comfort to
the saints in trouble.

Oh, grant us grace to bear whatever Thy righteous will puts upon us without repining ; and if business is going amiss, and if many things are cross to the desires of nature, may we feel it is Thy will, and, therefore joyfully yield to that will ; nay, more, may we take a delight in being stripped, if God strip us ; take a delight in smarting, if it be God who makes us smart. When Thou dost use the chisel upon these blocks of stone that are to be built upon the Living Stone, Lord, do not only square us, and fashion us, but separate us from the old rock to which we have been wedded so long : set us free from that hole of the pit, and let us be brought into the upper air, and built upon Christ, to lie there for ever.

Bless this our beloved church and its officers. We thank Thee for Thy mercy that many of us are spared to do service for Thee, notwithstanding many infirmities. We bless Thee for others, who having gone from us, have been brought back again ; for the many Sunday School teachers among us ; and ask that all may be anointed with fresh oil, that every working or suffering brother and sister may receive fresh grace this day ; that this may be a time of the trimming of lamps, that all may shine brightly to the praise of Thy grace.

Bless our country. The Lord in mercy avert the horrors of war from us. Grant that, by some means, peace may be continued, and war come to an end where it still rages; and oh, that the policy of truth and righteousness may once more be taken up in this land, and our nation be forgiven its great · national crimes.

Bless the Queen with every blessing, and all peoples that dwell on the face of the earth visit with the splendour of Thy love. "Let the people praise Thee, O God, yea, let all the people praise Thee: then shall the earth yield her increase, and God, even our own God, shall bless us. God shall bless us, and all the ends of the earth shall fear Him."

Forgive the weakness of our prayer, forgive the wandering of our heart: but through the Well-Beloved, who stands before Thee now in all His beauty as risen from the dead; through Him whom our soul loveth, even as Thou lovest Him; through Him whom we adore as "God over all, blessed for ever," though bone of our bone and flesh of our flesh—through Him and for His sake look kindly on us now! Amen and Amen.

SERMON: No. 1501.   (October 26, 1879.)

SCRIPTURE: Matt. vii.   HYMNS: 118 (Song ii.), 822, 381.

XVIII.

" YOUR ADVERSARY."

" Therefore rejoice, ye heavens, and ye that dwell in them. Woe to the inhabiters of the earth and of the sea ! for the devil is come down unto you, having great wrath, because he knoweth that he hath but a short time."—*Rev.* xii. 12.

———

GREAT God, we bless Thee that the battle between Thyself and the powers of darkness has never been uncertain. We praise Thy name that now it is for ever sure to end in victory. Our hearts this morning, amidst the struggles of the present day, would look back to the conflicts of Calvary, and see how our Lord for ever there broke the dragon's head. Oh that Thy people this morning might know that they are contending with a vanquished enemy, that they go forth to fight against one who, with all his subtlety and all his strength, has already been overthrown by Him who is our Covenant Head, our Leader, our Husband, our all.

Grant to Thy dear children who are by any means depressed because they feel the serpent at their heel, that that they may bless the name of Him whose heel was bruised before, but who in the very bruising broke the serpent's head. Our souls with songs of inward joy extol the mighty Conqueror. All honour and glory be unto Him who stood foot to foot with the Arch Enemy, but who was never wounded by him; the prince of this world came, but there was nothing in Thee, O Jesus, no tendency to sin, no turning aside; but Thou didst win from the first, even to the last, a glorious victory over this dread adversary of mankind. We see Thee now arrayed in Thy vesture dipped with blood, victorious over all Thy foes. Our spirit triumphs in the anticipation of the time when all thine enemies shall be destroyed, and death and hell shall be cast into the lake of fire, and God shall be all in all.

Oh that the time were come set for Thine advent, when the hidden shall be revealed, and the church of God shall no longer need her wings with which to fly, but shall come forth in all the glory with which Thy love arrays her, clothed with the sun and with the moon beneath her feet. Glory, and honour, and majesty, and power, and dominion, and might, be unto Him that sitteth upon the throne and unto the Lamb for ever and ever!

And now, we present ourselves before the throne of the great King to pay our reverence and homage there; for the Lord is God alone, and our heart doth worship Him intensely, reverently bowing unto the very dust before the Lord, for we are less than nothing, and Jehovah is all in all.

We would confess our many sins, with great self abhorrence and detestation of them. The Lord be pleased to forgive his servants in this thing, and let us each this morning feel the application of the precious "blood which speaketh better things than that of Abel." May every child of God know now that he is clean through the washing of the blood. Oh that we might be certain that no guilt is recorded against us now, for it is blotted out for ever and the record is destroyed. Being justified by faith may we have peace, deep, lasting peace with God, through Jesus Christ our Lord.

And Lord, wilt Thou be pleased to heal us of any wounds that we have received in the great conflict. Thou knowest that during the week some of us have been in the thick of the battle, and manifold temptations have gathered about us. If we have gathered aught of defilement, be pleased to put it away. If in converse with the world we have mired or dusted our feet, wash them, blessed Master, this morning, that we may be clean every whit. If our faith has suffered any damage, or our hope is not so bright as it was, or if our love to Thee be not as fervent as at one time it was; if the soul be sinking under the pressure of the fight in any degree, oh Thou whose every word is music, whose every promise is balm, whose every touch is life, draw near to the weary warrior now, and refresh us that we may rise again to the conflict, and never tire until the last enemy shall be beneath our feet, as beneath our Master's feet.

And O Lord, if it may please Thee, look upon any of Thy servants who are more than ordinarily tried, or who by reason of bodily weakness or the stress of severe trial, may specially need consolation, put under such the everlasting arms. So let the whole host be refreshed. Let those that lie in hospital be brought out of it and made whole; and as it is said of the host when Thou didst bring it out of Egypt, "there was not one feeble person in all their tribes," so may it be with us; may the weakest become as David, and David as the Angel of the Lord. Great Captain of the host, we ask this high favour of Thee on this Thy day, when Thine own are gathered together. Deny us not we beseech Thee.

And now, we ask Thee to give victory to Thy church all over the world. Oh look, Thou Mighty One, look down upon the heathen, and see how their gods stand riveted to their thrones. Cast them down, O Christ! Thou who hast cast out the dragon, cast down these inferior powers of darkness until not an idol god shall be left.

Thou seest also how the harlot of Babylon still sits upon her seven hills, and the multitudes wander after her. Oh that Thou wouldst cast her like a mill-stone in the flood and end her power for ever. And the " false prophet," too, whose power is waning, let it be utterly eclipsed; and oh that Christ might reign! The Lord grant it!

But sometimes we feel half staggered by the prayer, because our own dear land, and other lands where Christ is preached, are still so dark. Lord, look on countries where the gospel is proclaimed, and yet men live in sin, and the policy of many a state is unchristian, if not anti-christian. Oh look Thou on the nations; gather out the remnant of the woman's seed, even from among them, and let the light of Thy chosen shine forth, that it may be seen that Thy saints are not only lights to themselves but lights of the world, lights of the nations wherein they dwell.

Lord remember our great city: Oh, be not wroth very sore with it. Behold this day the gospel is preached, but the many turn their backs upon it. They might hear it, and they will not, and many that do hear it, reject it. The Lord raise up many voices yet that will be heard, that must be heard; and open men's ears; compel them to hear; yea, compel them to come into Thy marriage banquet, that Thy Son may have guests at His great feast of mercy.

The Lord bless us this day. Help us to be voices for God. Make this church to be full of such voices. May there be no silent member among us concerning the things of Christ; but may each one overcome through the blood of the Lamb and the word of His testimony.

O God, wilt Thou bless the various agencies carried on by us, that we may, as a church, help and do our part in the evangelisation of the world. We remember the many men who have been trained at our side, and are preaching to-day : the Lord speak through them. We remember the many brethren and sisters that will spend the great part of this day in endeavouring to bring others to Christ: the Lord prosper them all. Oh make us to be more and more a living church, a church in which God shall shew forth the glory of His power. Oh how we long for this ! May all ministries among us be living ministries, Holy Ghost ministries, and so may it be in all the churches, that every golden candlestick may have a candle well lit ; and may it come to pass that from the olive trees there shall pass into the golden pipes always sufficient of the sacred oil to keep the lights well burning to the glory of our God.

We cast ourselves upon Thee, and ask Thee to make us all useful to-day in our families, in our classes, in the church, in the world : and when Thou shalt have used us here, permit us the great joy of serving Thee day and night in Thy temple above.

One more prayer: it is, convert those who sit with us from Sunday to Sunday and are unconverted. Lord have mercy upon some that once were professors of religion, but continue to come in and out among us without repentance, without turning back to Him whom once they professed to know. Lord have mercy upon others that are hearers but hearers only, attentive hearers too, but not doers of the word. Oh save them speedily, bring them to Jesus. at once. We ask it for His dear name's sake. Amen.

SERMON : No. 1502.   (November 2, 1879.)
SCRIPTURE : Rev. xii.   HYMNS : 317, 335, 449.

XIX.

RISEN WITH CHIRST.

"If ye then be risen with Christ, seek those things which are above, where Christ sitteth on the right hand of God. Set your affection on things above, not on things on the earth."—*Col.* iii. 1, 2.

————.

OUR Father, we dare call Thee by that blessed name, for we feel the spirit of children. We have an earnest love to Thee, and an implicit trust in Thee; and we desire in all things to be obedient to Thy will, and to seek Thine honour. All our dependence is placed on Thee since the day when Thou didst teach us to believe in Jesus Christ: and now, Thou art all in all to us, Thou art our fulness, and we lose ourselves and find ourselves completely in Thee.

We would come to Thee this morning by the way which Thou hast appointed; and enabled by the Spirit whom Thou hast given, we would speak with Thee. Father, we are always grieving if more or less we offend against Thy holy mind; and we grieve ourselves, to think that we should grieve Thee. Our innermost desire is to be absolutely perfect. Oh how we wish we were! We hate every false way, and every sin; and we desire, with all the power of our mind, to be delivered from the dominion of any sin, and to be led into the blessed freedom of complete obedience to God.

Thou knowest Lord, for Thou searchest the heart and Thou triest the reins of the children of men—Thou knowest we can truly say, unless indeed we be under a very deep delusion, that we do wish to promote Thy glory among the sons of men; and that we count nothing to be riches, but that which makes us rich towards God; nothing to be health, but that which is sanity before the most High—holiness in Thy sight; and we reckon nothing to be pure, but what Thou hast cleansed; and nothing to be good, but that upon which Thy blessing rests. Yet Lord, though it be so, though our mind has been by Thy Spirit set towards holiness, there is a death within us; the old nature which strives against our life, and the members of the body often join with the corrupt nature within, to lead us astray. We swing towards holiness and then we seem like the pendulum, to swing the other way. We are wretched, because of this, and we cry out to Thee to deliver us. Oh that Thou wouldst deliver us!

We do thank Thee that Jesus gives us the victory; but we long to have that victory in ourselves more constantly realised—more perfectly enjoyed. We would lie in the very dust before Thee because of sin; and yet, at the same time, rejoice in the great Sin-bearer, that the sin is not imputed to us, that it is put away by His precious blood, that we are accepted in the Beloved. But even this does not content us ; we are crying after the work of the Holy Ghost within, till Satan shall be bruised under our feet, and sin shall be utterly destroyed.

Lord, Thou knowest the groanings of our heart ; our prayers cannot express them : but we bless Thee that there is One who maketh intercession for us, with groanings that cannot be uttered, who is with us, and dwelleth in us, and is promised to be with us for ever. We shall overcome, we shall win the victory, we shall rise superior to depression of spirit, we shall overcome the doubts, and fears, and tribulations of our inward heart, we shall overcome, for Christ doth lead the way and victory lies in His cross ; and we are sure of it, and therefore would we begin to sing the hymn of victory even now, saying— " thanks be unto God who causeth us always to triumph in every place, by Jesus Christ His Son."

At this time we would entreat Thee to visit us with Thy salvation. Lord we all want renewing, refreshing, reviving ; but there are some of Thy people that sink very low by reason of physical infirmity and mental suffering ; they lie in the very dust. But Lord, when our soul cleaveth to the dust, Thou canst still quicken us according to Thy word ; and we ask Thee to make this a red-letter day in our experience. May we renew our youth : may the love of our espousals come back to us : may the joy of our first days be restored : may the childlike faith of the first steps we ever took towards Christ, be given to us now ; and may we learn to rest in the Lord and wait patiently for Him.

O Lord our God, we do beseech Thee look upon the faint hearted and such as are swooning through affliction. Bring again from Bashan, yea bring up Thy people from the depths of the sea. Take away our mourning and give us music : remove our sackcloth and give us beauty : take away our sighs and fill our mouths with songs ; and let this be a radiant day of gladness, and a time of feasting from the Bridegroom's own hand ; and may our own spirits rejoice in Him with joy unspeakable and full of glory.

At this time also, great Father, wilt Thou visit this church with Thy great favour; and as Thou hast abounded toward us these many years in blessing, so give us now some new token, some fresh visitation for good. Lord Thou hast not always given summer weather to the field of nature, but spring comes on and summer returns. Oh give us summer weather as a church. May there be a great revival of religion in all the members, and especially in the minds of such as are growing cold or indifferent to holy things. Wherever there is any laxity of life, any slight holding of precious truth ; wherever the world is creeping in with its corroding influences ; wherever there is anything of sin which our eye sees not, but which Thine eye detects, be pleased to put it away. Fill the whole church with unity, with love, with life, with power.

We thank Thee for the many that are coming in among us fresh from the world. God be thanked for new converts ; may they be like fresh blood in the veins of the church, keeping her alive and keeping her active ; and may the spirit of the Lord come down upon pastors, and

elders, and deacons, Sunday School teachers and workers
and sufferers; and let the whole church be quickened.
Yea, and not this church only but all the little hills of
Zion, do Thou water with showers from on high. Let
the country churches receive a blessed visitation. Let all
the churches in foreign lands also be visited by the self-
same Comforter; and may there come to Thy church in
these dark and dreary days, bright shining after the rain.
May the time of the singing of birds come, and the voice
of the turtle be heard in our land!

And oh, whilst Thou art doing this, look on sinners!
Oh look on sinners! When Thou blessest Thy people,
Thou dost make them blessings. When the church is
vigorous, when the people praise Thee, then shall the
earth yield her increase, then shall all the nations praise
Thee too; for the joy of Zion is the joy of the whole earth,
when the Lord maketh glad His people then He maketh
the earth sit still and rest, or even if it rages, yet still
there is a time of salvation, a time of the ingathering of
the hidden ones, and Christ's name is glorious. But Lord
there is a great tumult in the world just now: we pray
Thee overrule it for Thy glory. Grant that the best ends
of progress, of truth and righteousness may be subserved;
and may it be seen still, that the Lord reigneth. Even
though the people should riot and rebel against the truth,
yet do Thou advance Thy cause; even by disaster and
defeat, if so it must be, or by success and prosperity. Let
Thy kingdom come, good Lord; let Thy kingdom come,
and let Thy will be done on earth as it is in heaven, and
our hearts shall sing with the angel choir, and be glad

with all the ransomed before the throne, because God is glorified. This is our soul's grandest object, that Jesus' name be lifted high, and His throne be set up among the people, to the praise of the glory of His grace. And now unto the Father, to the Son, and to the Holy Ghost, be glory, as it was in the beginning, is now and ever shall be, world without end. Amen.

SERMON : No. 1530. (March 28, 1880.)

SCRIPTURE : Col. ii. 8-23, iii. 1-15.   HYMNS : 306, 319, 873.

XX.

INTERCESSION FOR THE SAINTS.

" Likewise the Spirit also helpeth our infirmities: for we know not what we should pray for as we ought : but the Spirit itself maketh intercession for us with groanings which cannot be uttered. And he that searcheth the hearts knoweth what is the mind of the Spirit, because he maketh intercession for the saints according to the will of God."—*Rom.* viii. 26, 27.

———

OUR Father, we bless Thee that we dare use that name without a question ; for many of us feel the Holy Spirit bearing witness with our spirits that we are the children of God. We thank Thee that we have passed from death unto life, and have been begotten again unto a lively hope by the resurrection of Jesus Christ from the dead. He that sitteth on the throne, and maketh all things new, hath made us new, and called us into newness of life, and made us to feel a life within us which must outlast the ages, for it is the life of God.

Our Father, we would not crouch before Thee, like slaves before a tyrant, but feel the spirit of adoption, which shall draw us into familiar intercourse with Thee, though still with holy trembling, for Thou art God in heaven, and we are still but men upon the earth, and at the very sight of Thee we feel a trembling coming over us ; yet is there joy with it ; and Thou hast taught us to rejoice with trembling.

We would in spirit now pass into that inner place, into which the High Priest of Israel dared not come but once a year, and then not without blood. We bless Thee that the veil is rent ; and now every believer is made a priest, and permitted to come into the Holy of Holies, and to draw near unto the mercy-seat, all blood be-sprinkled, without fear of being regarded as an intruder, or smitten down like Nadab and Abihu.

O God, we stand, therefore, now in Thine immediate presence, and our very heart speaks to Thee, and we rejoice that Thou who searchest the heart, knowest what our heart would say ; and if these lips should fail to speak out the heart's utterances, Thou wilt interpret what is written in every bosom ; and if no lip this morning should express the desire of certain of Thy saints, because their groanings are such that they cannot utter them themselves, and, therefore, cannot expect anyone else to do it, yet Thou wilt read every heart ; for every heart is open before Thee as a book, and Thou readest the thoughts and intents of the heart.

And first, our Father, we would earnestly ask that every believer here may feel the power of the sprinkled blood most vividly and consciously. May we hear Jesus say by it, " Ye are clean, clean every whit " ; and may we have a sense of entire security, because Thou hast Thyself said it—" When I see the blood I will pass over you." This is the blood of our passover, and no destroying angel can touch us.

Now, Lord, next to this give each one of Thy children power to become the sons of God in their actions. May we become more and more like the First-born; may we begin to exercise our sonship by conquering ourselves. Help us to put down sin. May every sinful thought be driven out, and every thought be brought into captivity to the Spirit of God. Oh help us to be perfectly consecrated to Thy service, because we are the children of God. May we not live like children of the devil, neither serve him, nor serve our affections and lusts.

And, oh, grant us also to become sons by reason of the spirit of boldness that we shall feel. Give us not again the spirit of bondage that we may fear; but give us, we pray Thee, more and more of the spirit of adoption whereby we cry Abba, Father.

Lord, purify us! Thou hast pardoned; now purify, until every sin shall be destroyed within our hearts. We pray Thee hear the prayers of Thy children who also ask for strength and succour in their time of need. O Spirit of God help our infirmities. If we be pressed down with a load of sorrow; if we are in perplexity and know not what to do; if we are slandered and persecuted; if we in any way are made to feel the weight of the cross, help us, we pray Thee. Let not our weakness be staggered by that portion of our estate which comes under the head of tribulation. May we rather rejoice in infirmities, because the power of God doth rest upon us; and may

we glory in tribulations also, because these work in us, by
Thy good Spirit, all manner of holy graces to Thy
glory.

The Lord deliver His people from carking care ; and,
indeed, from caring about themselves! Oh for power to
roll our burden upon our God, and to sing all day long
because we are the Lord's, and He is ours. " The Lord
is our Shepherd : we shall not want. Surely goodness
and mercy shall follow us all the days of our life, and we
shall dwell in the house of the Lord for ever."

O Lord, make us a holy and a happy people. Help
us to live the separated life, and to tread it with firm and
brave step. Help us while we wrestle not with flesh and
blood, to fight with principalities, and powers, and
spiritual wickednesses in high places ; and may it be ours
to be made, by Thy Spirit, to triumph in every place,
being led in triumph by Thee from strength to strength,
from time to time, from age to age, till the history of
Thy whole church shall be one long triumph for the
conquering Lord. Glorify Thyself in us, we pray Thee,
even in these mortal bodies, and in our spirits which are
Thine.

Now would we put up most fervent and earnest
prayer for such who, as yet, do not know Thee. O Spirit
of God, convince men of sin, of righteousness, and of
judgment to come ; and especially convince the human
heart of the sin of not believing in the Lord Jesus Christ.
Oh make this to be very clear to the heart, that not
believing in Jesus is the highest act of enemity against
God. The rejection of God when He becomes man and

dies out of infinite love—surely this is the highest crime and misdemeanour against the great King. Oh that this might strike, like an arrow, into the heart of some. If they cannot accuse themselves of any gross sin of the body, yet may this grossest of all sins be laid, like a mill-stone, upon their conscience, that they have refused the Son of God and done despite to His precious blood; and how shall they escape if they neglect so great salvation!

O Spirit of God lay this home; and then convince them of righteousness. Let them see where righteousness is to be had, even in Christ! Let them know that righteousness is demanded of them; and, if they have it not from Christ, they will never have it, and they must perish in their sins.

And oh, Divine Spirit, set before them judgment to come. Let them tremble at the thought that Thou wilt come, that the great assize shall be held, and rebels against God and His Christ must be punished with eternal destruction from the presence of the Lord and from the glory of His power.

Thus bring the sinner to his knees; thus bring the conscience to tenderness; and then, sweet Spirit, reveal Jesus Christ to the troubled heart, and let there be the peace of God through faith. We have many things to pray for this morning, but, Lord, Thou knowest them all.

We specially pray for our country that God would bless it; and oh, that we might have a season·of revival of pure and undefiled religion in the land. We perceive that Thou canst turn the hearts of the people, as the trees of the wood are moved in the wind. Oh that there might come a deep searching of heart, great thoughtfulness of the Scriptures, reverence of God and the principles of justice and peace : and may this land make another stride in onward progress, and out of it may there be gathered a people whom Thou hast chosen, who shall show forth Thy praise.

With equal affection do we pray for all countries and lands ; and especially for that kindred nation where our own tongue is spoken, and our own God is worshipped. Oh Lord grant that these two great lands may go hand in hand together in the propagation of the gospel of Jesus Christ.

Lord, put down all false doctrine, all Popery, Mohamedanism and idolatry ; and may the day come in which Christ Himself shall be King among the nations, and His reign shall be inaugurated by the manifestation of His redeemed ; and unto Him be glory for ever and ever. Glory be unto the Father, and to the Son, and to the Holy Ghost, as it was in the beginning, is now, and ever shall be, world without end.   Amen.

SERMON : No. 1532.   (April 11, 1880.)

SCRIPTURE : Rom. viii. 14 to end.   HYMNS : 1009, 978, 460.

XXI.

THE SENTENCE OF DEATH IN OURSELVES.

" But we had the sentence of death in ourselves, that we should not trust in ourselves, but in God which raiseth the dead."— *2 Cor.* i. 9.

OUR Father, blessed be Thy name for ever and ever. Oh that we praised Thee more ! We must confess we never bless Thee as we ought, and our life is far too full of murmuring, or at the best too full of self-seeking, for even in prayer we may do this ; and there is too little of lauding, and adoring, and praising, and magnifying, and singing the high praises of Jehovah.

Oh God, wilt Thou teach us to begin the music of heaven ! Grant us grace to have many rehearsals of the eternal Hallelujah. " Bless the Lord, O my soul, and all that is within me bless His holy name." Grant us grace that we may not bring Thee blessings merely because Thou dost feed us, and clothe us, and because we receive so many mercies at Thy hand ; but may we learn to praise Thee even when Thou dost put us under the rod, and when the heart is heavy, and when mercies seem but scant. Oh that when the flocks are cut off from the stall, and there is no harvest, we may nevertheless rejoice in God.

Oh Lord, teach us this very morning the art of praise. Let our soul take fire, and like a censor full of frankincense, may our whole nature send forth a delicious perfume of praiseful gratitude unto the ever blessed One, Father, Son, and Holy Spirit.

Oh Lord, our chief desire this morning before Thee is to be right with Thee. Oh make us right with Thee, great Father. There are some in Thy presence who are not right with Thee at all ; Thy countenance they cannot behold, and Thou canst not accept their offering, for it is true of them, as of Cain, "sin lieth at the door." Oh God roll every sin away, but we know they must first feel the burden of it, they must come to Thee and confess it, they must accept the great Substitute and rest in Jesus. And our prayer shall be, Father, if our sin be not forgiven, we would put our head into Thy bosom and sob out, "Father, I have sinned against heaven and before Thee and am no more worthy to be called Thy son." Grant the kiss of forgiveness to each of Thy children this morning, and may we feel that Thou art faithful and just to forgive us our sins, and to cleanse us from all unrighteousness ; and in the joy of this, may we feel peace with Thee.

But Lord, many of us have been forgiven years ago. We have walked with Thee now, with holy joy and confidence, some of us for a quarter of a century, and others for more ; yet Lord there may be something between us and Thee even now, and if there be, "shew me wherefore Thou contendest with me." If Thou seest in Thy servants any wrong thing encouraged, any evil desire cherished; if there be anything that we delight in that Thou dost not delight in; if we have any habit which grieves Thee; if in anything we vex Thy Holy Spirit, our Father, forgive us our trespasses, as we forgive them that trespass against us; and then point out to us the trespass, and teach our feet to keep the ways of Thy commandments, and to trespass no more; for our heart is right towards Thy statutes and we desire holiness.

Oh we desire perfection. We know what it is to make a conscience of our every thought. We have looked upon every act of our lives and desired that in all things we might be conformed to Thy will, and Thou knowest this makes us walk very tenderly at times, and with much brokenness of spirit before Thee, because the more we look into our lives, the more we see to lament; and in proportion as Thou dost make us holy, in that very proportion do we spy out our unholiness, and find nests of sin where we never dreamt that the loathsome things had been. Father, cleanse us from secret faults. Purge us! Thou hast purged us with hyssop once, and we are clean; now wash us with water, even as Thou, blessed Jesus, didst wash Thy disciples' feet, and make us clean every whit, that we may be Thy priests and kings, sanctified wholly; and make us a people zealous of good works.

Bless, Lord, this our church, and let nothing spring up in this church that would grieve Thy Holy Spirit. We know that there are some among us that walk not after Thy commandments, some that grow cold, some that are negligent in prayer, some that add nothing to the strength

of Thy service.   But Lord, is it not so with all the
churches?   Oh wilt Thou not still continue to look upon
the faithful, and to make them yet more faithful; and to
look upon the wandering, and the backsliding, and to
restore them, lest they be an occasion of grief unto Thine
Israel, as Achan was who had hidden away the goodly
Babylonish garment, and the wedge of gold in his tent.

If Thou hast prospered any among us who may have
grown rich, and have forgotten the God who gave them
everything; or if Thou hast brought any into poverty and
in their poverty they have not acted as they should; or
if Thou hast left any brother to his own heart, and he
has found out that he is a fool; if any of us have grieved
Thee, oh lay not this sin to the charge of Thy church, and
lay it not to the charge of the offender either, but let a
sweet forgiveness be bestowed, let a restoration be granted
by Thy Spirit, and let the church be right with God.
Oh how we pray for this!

Lord, Thou hast not taken away Thy blessing from us.
We do rejoice in this: every day dost Thou aid us, and
this month Thou hast sent us perhaps more than ever—
glory be to Thy name!   And Thou dost provide for all
the work of the church, and send prosperity to it in every
part and quarter of it; and therefore do we fear and
tremble because of all the goodness which Thou dost
make to pass before us; and our heart is jealous with a
godly jealousy, lest in anything we should vex the Spirit
of God.   Oh Lord, grant us to be holy, grant us to be
accepted in the Beloved, and Thou shalt have all the
praise.

Now we have but one other prayer ; and that is, if we are right with Thee, help us to be right in all the transactions of daily life. Help us to be right with regard to Thy providential dealings with us. Lord give much patience to those that are tried. Give a holy resignation both to the sick and to the bereaved, and to such as are brought into poverty. Be very gracious to Thy dear children that they may never dishonor Thee when they are in affliction.

And wilt Thou keep Thy people right with regard to the world. Oh that the witness that we bear might be an unstained one. Oh grant to us to be a light in the world, that we may never cast darkness instead of light over the minds of men. Help us to live out Christ's life. Oh Lord, help us to be so consumed with zeal, that it may eat us up ; and may we be so full of love, that those who are round about us may know that if we write a harsh letter, or say a strong word, love alone dictates it. May we in everything be Christly, Godly; for God is love. Conquer our tempers, subdue our passions, rule us in body, soul, and spirit. Make us so to live that, when death shall close our life on earth, heaven itself, shall be but a continuance of the same life, because even now we have the beginnings of heaven in the earnest of the Spirit.

And now Lord, bless Thy universal church, and grant to it mercy and favour. Gather together Thine elect from under all heaven. Let the company of the faithful be accomplished, and the universal reign of Christ established.

Bless our own dear country.   God save and bless the Queen with every mercy ; and our rulers do Thou guide, uphold, sustain and direct.   Let them be guilty of no folly ; but the Lord teach our senators wisdom.

And may it please Thee Lord, to bless other countries too ; especially those lands which love our common Christ, and speak our mother tongue ; and, indeed, all the nations where Jesus Christ is known, do Thou visit with a revival   And heathen, and Mahometan, and Popish lands ; Oh let the light break in upon their midnight, let the day dawn and Christ be glorified.

What more can we ask : we ask all in His dear name, dear to us and dear to Thee, Oh our Father : and unto the Father, to the Son and to the Holy Ghost be glory everlasting.   Amen.

SERMON : No. 1536.   (May 2, 1880.)

SCRIPTURE : 2 Cor. i.   HYMNS : 125, 624, 741.

XXII.

INTERCESSION FOR ONE ANOTHER.

" Moreover as for me, God forbid that I should sin against the Lord in ceasing to pray for you : but I will teach you the good and the right way."—1 *Sam.* xii. 23.

———

GOD of Israel, God of Jesus Christ, our God for ever and ever ; help us now by the sacred Spirit, to approach Thee aright with deepest reverence, but not with servile fear ; with holiest boldness, but not with presumption. Oh teach us as children to speak to the Father, and yet, as creatures to bow before our Maker.

Our Father, we would first ask Thee whether Thou hast ought against us as Thy children. Have we been asking somewhat of Thee amiss, and hast Thou given us that which we have sought ? We are not conscious of it, but it may be so ; and now we are brought, as an answer to our presumptuous prayers, into a more difficult position than the one we occupied before. It may be that some creature comfort is nearer to us than our God. We had better have been without it, and have dwelt in God, and have found our joy in Him. But now, Lord, in these perilous circumstances, give us grace that we may not turn away from Thee. If our position now be not such as Thou wouldst have allotted to us, had we been wiser, yet nevertheless grant that we may be taught to behave ourselves aright, even now, lest the mercies Thou hast given should become a cause of stumbling, and the obtaining of our heart's desire, should become a temptation to us.

Rather this morning do we feel inclined to bless Thee for the many occasions in which Thou hast not answered our prayer, for Thou hast said that we did ask amiss, and therefore we could not have ; and we desire to register this prayer with Thee, that whensoever we do ask amiss Thou wouldst in great wisdom and love be pleased to refuse us. O Lord if we at any time press our suit, without a sufficiency of resignation, do not regard us we pray Thee ; and though we cry unto Thee day and night, concerning anything, yet, if Thou seest that herein we err, regard not the voice of our cry we pray Thee. It is our heart's desire in our coolest moments, that this prayer might stand on record as long as we live,—" Not as I will, but as Thou wilt."

But, oh Lord, in looking back, we are obliged to remember with the greatest gratitude, the many occasions in which Thou hast heard our cry. We have been brought into deep distress, and our heart has sunk within us, and then have we cried to Thee, and Thou hast never refused to hear us. The prayers of our lusts Thou hast rejected, but the prayers of our necessities Thou hast granted ; not one good thing hath failed of all that Thou hast promised. Thou hast given us exceedingly abundantly above what we asked, or even thought; for there was a day when our present condition would have been regarded as much too high for us ever to reach; and, in looking back, we are surprised that those who did lie among the pots of Egypt, should now sit every man under his vine and fig tree; that those who wandered in the wilderness, in a solitary way, should now find a city to dwell in; that we who were prodigals in rags, should now be children in the Father's bosom; that we who were companions of swine, should now be made heirs of God and joint heirs with Jesus Christ.

Oh what encouragement we have to pray to such a prayer-hearing God, who far exceeds the requests of His children! Blessed be the name of the Lord for ever; our inmost heart is saying, Amen, blessed be His name! If it were only for answered prayer, or even for some unanswered prayers, we would continue to praise and bless Thee as long as we have any being.

And now Lord, listen to the voice of Thy children's cry this morning. Wherever there is a sincere heart seeking for greater holiness, answer Thou that request; or wherever there is a broken spirit seeking for reconciliation with Thyself, be pleased to answer it now. Thou knowest where there is prayer, though it be unuttered, and even the lips do not move. Oh hear the publican who dares not lift his eyes to heaven; hear him while he cries, " God be merciful to me, a sinner." Hear such as seem to themselves to be appointed unto death. Let the sighing of the prisoner come before Thee. Oh that Thou wouldst grant peace and rest to every troubled spirit within this house ; ay, and to all such all over the world, who now desire to turn their faces to the cross, and to see God in Christ Jesus reconciling them unto Himself.

O Lord, if there are any of Thy servants exercised about the cases of others, we would thank Thee for them. Raise up in the church many intercessors, who shall plead for the prosperity of Zion, and give Thee no rest till Thou establish her, and make her a joy in the land.

There are some of us that cried to Thee about our country. Thou knowest how in secret, we groaned and sighed over evil times ; and Thou hast begun to hear us already, for which we desire to praise and bless Thy name. But we would not cease to pray for this land, that Thou wouldst roll away from it all its sin. That Thou wouldst deliver it from the curse of drunkenness, from infidelity, from popery, from ritualism, from rationalism, and every form of evil ; and that this land might become a holy land. O Lord bring the multitudes of the working men to listen to the gospel. Break in, we pray Thee, upon their stolid indifference ; for how many there are of them who have not yet risen from their beds this morning, who have not thought of coming up to any place of worship—Lord give them a love to Thy house, a desire to hear Thy gospel.

And then wilt Thou look upon the poor rich who, so many of them, know nothing about Thee, and are worshipping their own wealth. The Lord grant that the many for whom there are no special gospel service, but who are wrapped up in self-righteousness, might be brought to hear the gospel of Jesus, that they also, as well as the poor, might come to Christ. God bless this land with more of gospel light; with more of gospel life and love. Thou wilt hear us O Lord !

Then would we pray for our children, that they might be saved. Some of us can no longer pray for our children's conversion : our prayers are heard already ; but there are others who have children who vex them, and grieve their hearts. O God save sons and daughters of godly people. Let them not have to sigh over their children as Eli did, and as Samuel did ; and may they see their sons and daughters become the children of the living God.

We would pray for our servants, for our neighbours, for our kinsfolk of near or far degree, that all might be brought to Jesus. Do Thou this, O God, of Thine infinite mercy !

And as we are now making intercession ; we would, according to Thy word, pray for all kings and such as are in authority, that we may lead quiet and peaceable lives. We pray for all nations also. O Lord bless and remember the lands that sit in darkness; and let them see a great light ; and may missionary enterprise be abundantly successful.

And let the favoured nations, where our God is known, especially this land, and the land across the mighty ocean, that love the same Saviour and speak the same tongue, be always favoured with the divine presence, and with abundant prosperity and blessing. O Lord, Thou hast chosen this our race, and favoured it and multiplied it on the face of the earth ; and whereas with its staff it crossed this Jordan, it hath now become two great nations.

Lord be pleased to bless the whole of this race, and those absorbed into it; and then all other races, that in us may be fulfilled the blessing of Abraham. " I will bless you, and ye shall be a blessing."

And now, Father, glorify Thy Son! In scattering pardon through His precious blood, glorify Thy Son! In sending forth the eternal Spirit to convince men, and bring them to His feet, Father, glorify Thy Son! In enriching Thy saints with gifts and graces, and building them up into His image, Father, glorify Thy Son! In the gathering together of the whole company of His elect, and in the hastening of His kingdom, and His coming, Father, glorify Thy Son! Beyond this prayer we cannot go. Glorify Thy Son, that Thy Son also may glorify Thee; and unto Father, Son, and Holy Spirit be glory for ever and ever. Amen.

SERMON : No. 1537. (May 9, 1880)

SCRIPTURE : 1 Sam. xii. 1-23.　　　HYMNS : 177, 972, 958.

XXIII.

THE DISCIPLE WHOM JESUS LOVED.

"Then Peter, turning about, seeth the disciple whom Jesus loved following; which also leaned on his breast at supper, and said, Lord, which is he that betrayeth Thee?"—*John* xxi. 20.

———

OUR Father, which art in heaven, Thou art infinitely beyond the grasp of our understanding; but in great condescension, Thou hast brought Thyself very near to the grasp of our love, and we trust this morning many of us can say with all sincerity, "Thou knowest all things. Thou knowest that I love Thee."

O Lord, it has seemed to us impossible not to love Thee; for Thou art so supremely lovable, so full of goodness, so perfect. Thou hast manifested Thyself to us as love, and shall not love go out towards love? Especially this morning do we feel our hearts warmed towards Thee, in the person of Thy dear Son. Surely we cannot see Him made our brother, bone of our bone, and flesh of our flesh, sympathising with us, married to us, dead for us and risen again for us—we cannot gaze into His right royal face, without feeling our heart melt at the very sight of Him. Oh Jesus we love Thee—we are

Thine ; and Thou art ours.   Thou hast given Thyself to us, as well as for us ; and now we cheerfully give ourselves back to Thee, feeling that we are never so much our own, as when we are Thine ; that indeed we are not ourselves, until we are lost in Thee ; but that then have we found our truest manhood, when it and all else is surrendered to the all-conquering power of Jesus Christ our Lord.

We come a second time to Thee in public worship this morning, with the same prayer with which we commenced—it is the prayer for love.   We have expressed our love, but we are ashamed when we have done so, because after all what is our love ? it is so faint, so cold to Thee, compared with Thy love to us.   So we would adore Thee this morning for the love which Thou hast manifested to us.   Thou didst love us before the foundation of the world : Thine is no new compassion; for whom Thou didst foreknow, Thou didst predestinate to be conformed unto the image of Thy Son, out of Thine own pure love to them : and because Thou hast loved us with an everlasting love, therefore with lovingkindness hast Thou drawn us, and we feel the drawings now.

Thou didst first pluck us like brands out of the burning.   We remember well when Thou didst draw us from a corrupt world, and from our own self-righteousness, and we came to Jesus.   But Thou art drawing still: we feel the sacred bands ; we yield to them, glad to do so. Lord, draw us this morning upward to Thyself, nearer than ever.   May we not be satisfied with those heights of devotion to which we have attained; but may we reach somewhat higher to-day.   Oh that we might become

more completely consecrated! May the image of Christ
become more perfect upon us, stamp it deeper into our
nature. We trust the image is there; but oh that it set
still deeper into our very selves, that all might see that
the seal of the Holy Ghost was upon us, in the likeness
of Christ our Lord.

Our Father, wilt Thou be pleased to-day to fill us with
delight because of Thy love. Are we heavy of heart—let
Thy sweet love lighten the burden; for what after all can
there be to trouble the man whom God loves? Shall we
not find even in Thy rod a sweetness, as Jonathan did,
when he dipped his rod in the honey? Hast Thou not
said, "as many as I love I rebuke and chasten," shall
we not therefore take Thy rebukes, and chastenings, and
even rejoice in them, because therein the love of God is
manifested toward us.

Are Thy dear children poor, or are they sick in body,
or are they losing those they love, or is there yet a newly
digged grave over which they could shed floods of tears?
Oh sweet love of God, comfort them. Cover all the
rocks, O mighty tide of everlasting love, till not a rock is
seen, and on that glassy sea may our spirits float above
the rocks, which else had wrecked our lives. We do pray
Thee give us comfort, but also give us strength as well as
consolation.

Lord, we are very weak, and in ourselves we have no
desire to be otherwise, because when we are weak, then
are we strong; but we are very strong in Thee, and we do
wish to have faith to perceive this. Lord, some of Thy
children think Thee weak, because they are; and suppose

that grace will fail them, because the flesh does: but oh
teach them better, and may they know that it is just in
the death of the creature, that they shall find the life of
God revealed.

Oh that our spirit might be always subject to the
Divine Spirit: may its earthiness and feebleness, only
reveal the heavenliness, and the strength of the indwelling
Spirit of God. And oh grant us to feel that we have
power to overcome sin; that we have power to resist the
lusts of the flesh, and to despise the pomp of the world,
and the lust of the eyes. Though we groan within ourselves concerning the body of this death, yet sing we also
" thanks be unto God that giveth us the victory through
Jesus Christ our Lord." Help Thy children to take the
victory, to rejoice that they do conquer; yea that we are
more than conquerors, through Him who hath loved us.

And now that we are asking Thee to let Thy love be
revealed to us in all its sweet influences; and now that
we ask also that our love to Thee may be fervent, we pray
Thee make us useful to our brethren. O Lord, we would
not live unto ourselves; make us serviceable in gathering
in the lost sheep. Make us wise that we may go after
them in their devious wanderings, and discover them.

Lord, help us to speak a word in season to him that is
sad of heart. When Thine arrows stick fast in the
conscience, may we know how to apply the balm of Jesus'
wounds. Make us ready to tell out the sweet gospel which
has been so precious to our own souls; and as men that
have newly come ourselves from the presence of a
pardoning Saviour—men but newly washed in that dear

blood which maketh white as snow, may we go and tell to
our fellow-men, all black as they are, how they also can
be made whiter than snow.

Lord, make us useful to Thine own children that have
backslidden.   May we be as Peter was to whom Thou
saidst, "when Thou art converted strengthen Thy
brethren."   O Lord, make us useful among backsliders—
this very day may some of us be enabled to do somewhat
toward the fetching up of the rear guard, of those that
loiter and linger, that the whole army of Christ may
quicken its pace and march to victory.

And now, Lord Jesus, we have a thousand things to
ask of Thee, and of Thy Father; but Thou knowest what
we have need of before we ask.   Give to each one of Thine
own that special gift most needed: we may not even know
what it is, but according to Thine own wisdom and
prudence, deal out of Thy treasury things new and old,
for the enrichment and comfort of Thy people.

Bless this our beloved church: keep them still in
unity and earnestness of heart.   In all fresh advances
that we hope to make, be with us and help us.

Bless our dear orphan children, let them all be Thine.
Help us in the building of new houses for orphan girls,
and provide for our necessities in that matter.

Bless the dear sons of this church, trained at our own
side, who go forth to preach the gospel : whether they be
in the College, or whether they are preaching outside of it,
let the blessing of the Lord be with every one of them.

And all those who go from house to house with books,
seeking to speak a word in season to the neglected ; do

Thou help them, and make this church still to be the fruitful mother of children.   Yea make every one of us useful to Thy glory.

All other churches do Thou remember with even a greater blessing.   Let all the churches of Jesus Christ on the continent, as well as in this island, and far away in America and in all our distant colonies, all be revived and refreshed.   Yea, and those that speak not our tongue— those advanced posts among the heathen; do Thou remember them favourably, and visit them graciously.

Oh that the time were come when war shall cease, when drunkenness shall be put away, when all cruelty shall be abolished, when every superstition shall come to an end, and all oppression of man by man.   When shall it be, save when He cometh, whose right it is to reign? At the very thought of His coming our spirits begin to glow and burn with lofty hopes.   Come quickly ; even so, come quickly Lord Jesus.   "Let the whole earth be filled with His glory.   Amen and Amen."

SERMON : No. 1539.   (May 23, 1880.)

SCRIPTURE : 1 John ii.   HYMNS; 810, 784, 798.

XXIV.

FREE GRACE, AND FREE-GIVING.

"Now our Lord Jesus Christ himself, and God, even our Father, which hath loved us, and hath given us everlasting consolation and good hope through grace. Comfort your hearts, and stablish you in every good word and work."—2 *Thess.* ii. 16, 17.

———

GLORIOUS Lord God; our faith is fully assured of Thy being, and our heart rejoices in Thine infinite love. Blessed was the day when first we knew our God. We mourn and lament with deep penitence, that we should have lived so long strangers to our best friend, to Him in whose hand our breath is, and whose are all our ways. It is of Thy grace that we were ever brought to know Thee. Had we been left to ourselves we should have wandered on, and have remained in darkness till this day; but blessed be Thy name, O Thou God of all grace, Thou hast revealed Thyself to us, Thou hast brought Thy life to our death, and made us alive in Thee; Thou hast brought Thy light to our blindness, and made us to behold Thee; and now Thou art not only the greatest source of joy to our spirit, but Thou art all our joy—we have none apart from Thee. Whatever of comfort we find in the creature, we know it is but fickle; and while it is there, it comes from Thee, for all these things are empty, and vain, and void without Thee. Whom have we in heaven but Thee, and there is none upon earth that we desire beside Thee !

And Lord, we bless Thee for ever teaching us the way of faith ; for enabling us to cast our guilty souls upon the Divine propitiation, made in Christ Jesus ; for peace, like a river, has streamed into our spirit ever since. We bless Thee for the power to trust Thee with everything else, for time as well as for eternity. We are sure we never live except as we live by faith ; that all else is but death, and the counterfeit of life. Lord God, Thou hast written death before our eyes on all the creature ; Thou hast made us see the vanity of the most substantial things on earth. Behold we walk as in a vain show, and we disquiet ourselves in vain. All things are but shadows ; but Thou, Thou art the eternal all. Casting our anchor upon Thee we are stedfast, and fixed, and safe ; but all things else are quicksands. We cannot, dare not, find comfort, nor make a hope of them. Thou, Lord, art all our expectation, all our salvation, and all our delight ; and this morning, in the act of public devotion, we would cry, " Only my soul waiteth upon God, for my expectation is from Him."

Now this day, be pleased, in infinite mercy by Christ Jesus, to visit Thine assembled people. Give us first a sense of perfect pardon. May there be nothing between any child of Thine and Thyself, great Father, that could mar the perfection of communion. May we know that Thou hast forgiven us for Jesus Christ's sake. And as for anything in us that would grieve Thy Spirit, take it away at once, and then let Thy Spirit bear witness with our spirit that we are the children of God. Oh now give us the spirit of adoption. If indeed we be Thine, by Thy Fatherly love to us, we do beseech Thee breathe into every child of Thine a sense of love, a sense of Thy near presence.

And then Lord, wilt Thou deal with us according to Thy wisdom and prudence. Take out of us every evil and false way: aught wherein we have deceived ourselves do Thou remove. Anything which looks like growth in grace, which is mere puffing up do Thou take away; aught which we prize, which is but counterfeit, do Thou utterly destroy: and oh, bring us of Thy great love to know Christ in truth, that what we know we may know, and not think we know. And oh that there might be a deep reality about our Christian experience, and knowledge; that the truth of God may be incarnate in the truth which lives in us.

Dear Saviour, Thou knowest the peculiar trials and conditions of all these Thy people; and, we do pray Thee, now deal with each child of Thine according to his special need. Great Physician walk this hospital. Come and look on each special case, and may there be a masterpiece of Thy heavenly surgery in the case of each one of us.

Many of us need comfort; our heart is cast down within us. There are many of Thy saints in whose soul deep calleth unto deep at the noise of Thy waterspouts. Command Thy lovingkindness this morning, and let Thy song be with us at this moment. Up from the shades may we ascend into the eternal light. Oh that the sun of Thy love might shine full on our brows, till our faces shall be bright like the face of Moses!

Oh that we might have such fellowship with God this morning, that we might defy Satan, defy unbelief, defy the flesh, defy the world, with a holy joy which comes not of the creature, and which the creature cannot mar—a "joy unspeakable and full of glory," a draught out of the eternal fountains which well up from the deep which lieth under in the immutable and everlasting love and decree of God. Oh, let it be so with every child of Thine at this good hour.

Now we do, with all our hearts, pray Thee to gather in the rest of Thy family who, as yet, are far off from Thee. O mighty grace, seek out the prodigal! O mighty love, receive the prodigals when they come back! O mighty grace change their hearts and make them to love the great Father.

We do pray for all who are out of the way; for such in this congregation as remain unsaved. Lord, let them not die in their sins. Have mercy upon some that have had a godly training, but remain ungodly. Oh condemn them not, we pray Thee, with such a mass of guilt upon them; but save them yet. Lord, have great mercy upon such as are ignorant of Christ, and therefore sin, but know not what they do. Let them become trophies of Thy wondrous love. Gather them in; oh, gather them in to-day.

Now Thy servant, with a full heart, desires to bless Thee for the continual increase which Thou dost make to this church. Thou hast refreshed our soul by the testimonies of many that have lately found the Saviour. Blessed be the Lord, the Holy Ghost, who hath not suffered the word to fall to the ground, but who hath added to the church daily of such as shall be saved. Lord, continue this great favour. Stir up our dear brethren and sisters to continual prayer for a blessing. May the fire on this altar never go out; but as we have enjoyed, these many years, an unexampled prosperity, oh that we might continue to enjoy it still, unworthy though we be. Still, Lord, help us in every holy word and work.

Prosper us in the enterprises to which we set our hands. Bless our young man that go forth from us to preach the word. Blessed is the man that hath his quiver full of them. May there be many such reared up in this church that shall preach Christ crucified. Give to the church more and more the spirit of evangelisation, and may many young men in the church, that are now sitting still and quiet, be moved to preach even in the streets, the unsearchable riches of Christ.

Lord renew the zeal of the church towards the Sabbath school. May there be more coming forward to give themselves to the training of the young for Christ. Oh say to many a Peter, " Feed My lambs."

Revive the church of God in every place, we beseech Thee, in this dear isle of ours, so highly favoured; and on the continent, and among our beloved brethren in America and Australia. Let the kingdom of Jesus Christ spread in all countries. Let Thy kingdom come, great God, ay let it come speedily.

It doth not trouble us to think that Christ shall come ; it is indeed our joy. Make no tarrying, oh our Lord ! But meanwhile make us watchful, earnest, active ; and may we be as good servants, whose loins are girt, and whose lamps are trimmed. May we wait for the Master till He cometh.

Now give a blessing this morning : we come back to that prayer of ours—a blessing to each one. Bless me, even me also, O my Father ! The prayer is offered in the name of Jesus Christ the Mediator. Amen.

SERMON : No. 1542.   (June 13, 1880.)

SCRIPTURE : 2 Thess. i. ii. 1-4.   HYMNS : 728, 694, 248.

XXV.

AN EVENING PRAYER.

" But without faith it is impossible to please him : for he that cometh to God must believe that he is, and that he is a rewarder of them that diligently seek him."—Heb. xi. 6.

———

OUR Father, our faith is in Thee; our expectation is from Thee; our love goeth out towards Thee; we believe Thee; we accept every word of Thy sacred revelation as being eternal verity and immutable truth. Sometimes we are troubled to know whether the promises are for us—whether we really have a share in covenant blessings; but we thank Thee that Thou hast helped many of us to hold a trial in the court of conscience, and since our heart condemns us not we have confidence towards God. Let this be the portion of all Thy children. May we come away from doubting and fearing and hesitating, and may we believe. Oh, for the faith which trusts the bare promise of God! Let us not be asking for signs and wonders, and withholding faith because these are not given to us; but whatsoever we find in Thy word may we believe it to be sure truth, and hang our

souls upon it.   Above all things, give us grace to trust in
Jesus, in the full atonement made, and the utmost
ransom paid.   " He is all my salvation and all my
desire " : may we each one be able to say this of Him who
" of God is made unto us wisdom, righteousness, sanctification, and redemption."

> " Thou, O Christ, art all we want ;
> More than all in Thee we find."

Oh, let us never mistrust Thee, Thou blessed Son of
God.   May we have no doubt about Thy Father's
love—no suspicion as to the love of the Spirit ; but may
we joy in God by Jesus Christ, through whom also we
have received the atonement.   May we come to anchor,
and, casting anchor in the port of peace, may we never be
troubled again about that question, but be able to say
" My Father " with an unfaltering lip.   The Lord grant
that we may all of us have not only faith in Christ, but
full assurance of faith, whereby we shall trust, for the
present and for the future, everything in those dear hands
that were nailed to the cross for us.   Help Thy children
to perform an act of faith to-night by leaving all their
troubles apart and coming close to their Lord.   He has
sweat great drops for us, and now Thou biddest Thine
own children to cease therefrom, even as of old Thou
badest the priests to wear no garment that caused sweat,
because they were to find rest in Thy service and peace
in the performance of their holy duties.   Even so may
Thy people do.

O Lord God, even while we have been reading that
chapter, of which some are so much afraid, we have felt

that we could well trust Thee with a boundless sovereignty, and we do. Thou art so good, so kind, so just, so holy, that no mistake is possible to Thee. Thou art the fountain and source of all law : what Thou commandest it is ours to obey. We have heard the thunder of that sentence, "Nay, but O man, who art thou that repliest against God?"; and in meekness of heart and lowliness of spirit we bow before the infinite glory of Thy majesty, and it is to us the most joyful of all songs, "The Lord reigneth : let the earth rejoice. Let the multitudes of the isles be glad thereof."

Lord, we yield up to Thy sovereignty all that we are and all that we have. Do as Thou wilt with us. Whenever our wishes grow into willings, and our willings become obtrusive fault-findings with Thy providence, have mercy upon Thy servants in this thing, and take away from us the evil heart of unbelief that dares to question Thee. Be this the finale of our every prayer, "Nevertheless, not as I will, but as Thou wilt;" and be this the great pleading of our heart every day, "Thy kingdom come; Thy will be done on earth as it is in heaven." O Thou who art God, we have heard Thee say, "Be still and know that I am God;" and what a silence hast Thou made in our heart, where else there had been murmuring and complaint, when we have understood "The Lord hath done it." Aaron held his peace when he knew this; and so would we. Nay, we would do more. We would speak out of our griefs and our down-castings, and say, "The Lord gave, and the Lord hath taken away. Blessed be the name of the Lord. Though

He slay me, yet will I trust in Him, for the Lord is good to Israel, even to such as are of a clean heart. Blessed be His name."

And now, our Father, hear the pleadings of Thy children as we thus bow before Thee and yield everything to Thy parental will. Now bless Thy children. Sanctify us, Lord, spirit, soul, and body. Cleanse us even as with hyssop. Cleanse us in our inward parts, and make us to know wisdom in the secret places of our spirit.

And, Lord, wilt Thou also help such of Thy children as are very sorely burdened. When Thou layest on a burden, give strength equal to it, and if the burden should press heavier and heavier, hold the everlasting arms yet more consciously underneath us. Remember some present who have lately been bereaved. They lately had the sentence of death in themselves by reason of sore disease of body. Help, strengthen, comfort, deliver. The widow and the fatherless are always Thy care. Look, most tender and compassionate Lord, upon all such as are in any trouble of mind, or body, or estate; and let the rich comforts of the Comforter Himself be dispensed to them.

And, Lord, wilt Thou keep those that are not troubled. Let them rejoice with trembling. Wilt Thou preserve us all from any of the intoxication that comes of prosperity, and when our heart is glad, if it be not with the high joy that comes of God, let us always look to Thee to sober us in such moments. The Lord lead us safely on to His eternal kingdom. We will not ask whether the road will be rough or smooth. We leave that with Thee; only bring us to behold the face of Him we love. If Thou wilt give us bread to eat and raiment to put on, and bring us to our Father's house in peace, it is all we ask below. Whatsoever Thy will ordains, only do bring us to our Father's house in peace. Grant us this.

Father, one other prayer: it is that Thou wouldest bless those that do not know Thee. We pray Thee that we may have in our own hearts much of the heaviness that Paul knew, when we think of the many ungodly ones, especially of those that are of our own kith and kin, such as have heard the gospel from their very childhood, in whose father's house there was a prophet's chamber, whose mother died with the name of Jesus on her lips, whose father, grown grey with age, is on the road to glory, and they are still unconverted. Oh, bring them in! Dear Father, there are many of us praying now from the bottom of our hearts that all our children may be Thy children, and that all related to us may be of the family of Christ. Then, Lord, we thank Thee for that blessed word, "The promise is unto you and to your children;" but Thou didst not stop there, for Thou hast said, "and to them that are afar off, even to as many as the Lord our God shall call." Lord, bring in the far-off ones. Save poor fallen women : save the equally fallen men.

Oh God, have mercy upon heathen lands; upon Popish countries; upon those that sit in the Mahometan moon-darkness. The Lord be pleased to let His light shine over all the sons of men, and accomplish the number of His redeemed, to the praise of the glory of His grace wherein He hath made us accepted in the Beloved. And to Father, Son, and Holy Spirit be glory, as it was in the beginning, is now, and ever shall be, world without end. Amen.

SUNDAY EVENING, August 20, 1885. SCRIPTURE: Rom. ix.

HYMNS: 734, 623, 624.

XXVI.

AN EVENING PRAYER.

"Herein is love, not that we loved God, but that he loved us, and sent his Son to be the propitiation for our sins."— 1 *John* iv. 10.

————

GLORIOUS God, there are many of us who can bless Thee that we know Thee. There was a time when we lived in Thy world but had never known the Creator. We were partakers of Thy providence, but we did not know the Provider. We went up and down in the sunlight, but we were blind. There were voices all around us, but we were deaf to all things spiritual. And some of us lived in this way for years. Some in Thy presence are in that way this evening. They know not God: neither do they desire the knowledge of Thy ways. They can see and understand many things, but they do not desire to know Him in whom they live and move and have their being. It was a happy day for us when, in the infinite sovereignty of Thy love, Thou didst look upon us and call us by Thy grace. Then did the dead heart begin to beat. Then did light enter the darkened eye, and then we turned to Thee. It was the best discovery we had ever made when we found that there was, after all, a God, ready to hear us, willing to listen to our cries. But, Lord, at the first this great discovery caused us

much pain, for we found in our hearts an enmity to Thee,
a natural alienation; and we found that we had grieved
Thee, that we had vexed Thy spirit by sin. We admire
Thee all the more for this, for we would not care for a
God who did not hate sin. Oh, with what reverence we
fell at Thy feet even when we heard Thee speak in
tones of thunder, and say, "The soul that sinneth, it
shall die." When Thy grace had really made us to
know Thee, Thy justice, terrible as it was, had our
submissive reverence. We felt that, if our souls were
sent to hell, righteousness and justice would approve it
well. O God, we remember how we lay at Thy feet.
Our thoughts were as a case of knives cutting our hearts;
and then didst Thou come to us, and Thou didst make
known Thy love. O blessed day in which Thou didst
reveal Thyself dressed in the silken robes of love!
When we saw that Jesus died that we might live, that
the cross was the best proof of divine affection, then we
looked to Jesus suffering in our stead. We trusted in
the great atonement, and we found a peace. O, what
shall we say of it? Our very soul doth sing at the
remembrance of the peace which has never been taken
from us. Many days have passed since first we knew it,
and many changes we have seen, but we have never
lost our hold on Christ; nor has He ever lost His
hold of us ; and here we are still, to weep to the praise
of the mercy that we have found, and to tell to others, as
we have breath to speak, that the Lord is a great sin-
pardoning God. There is none like Him, passing by
transgression, iniquity, and sin, and, for Jesu's sake,

receiving the vilest of the vile to His bosom, and casting out none that come unto Him ; taking up even the blasphemer and the drunkard, yea, the very worst, and washing even these from their crimson sins and making them whiter than newly-fallen snow.   O Lord, we sometimes wish that we could sing like cherubim and seraphim.   Then would we praise Thee better.   But as it is, human voices are all we have, but they shall be used to the praise of "free grace and dying love," to which we owe all that we have, and all we ever hope to have.

Now, Lord, to-night bless this people.   O my Lord, bless these dear friends from whom I have been separated for a while.   Bless and prosper them.   Let those that fear Thy name be happy in Thee while we are preaching to-night.   May those who are truly thine, have a joyous and happy season.   May they rejoice in the great love of God, and feel their souls overflow with delight at their remembrance of it.

But, oh, we beseech Thee, especially save souls to-night.   Make up for our ten dumb Sabbaths.   Give us to-night ten times as much—nay, it must be eleven times as much : we cannot afford to lose this one.   Oh, give us eleven times as much blessing as we have ever had before.   May many, many, many be brought out of darkness into marvellous light, and delivered from the prison-house into the liberty of Christ.

Lord, there are some here that have heard us many times, and yet Thou hast not spoken to their hearts effectually.   Oh, speak to-night.   Take them in hand, great Lord.   They shall be made willing in the day of Thy power.   Oh, that this might be the day of Thy power !   There are others who are quite strangers to this house, and perhaps to the gospel.   May the new note strike them.   From the silver cornet of the gospel may there come to them a sound unknown before, which shall reach their very soul ; and may they answer to it. Bid them come to Christ and live to-night.   O divine love, sweetly draw them.   Cast the bands of love about them, and the cords of a man, and draw them to Thyself. Young men and young women, ay, and old men and old women,—draw them to Thyself, most divine Lord; and may there be many trophies to the power of the gospel to-night.   All our prayer is now before Thee.   We wish everybody in the house to be saved.   The Lord grant it, for Christ's sake.   Amen.

Sunday Evening, Jan. 30th, 1887.   Scripture : Gen. xxii.

Hymns : 199, 782, 288.

KEEP IN MERCY'S WAY.

—o—

Let sermons and prayers be thy delight, because they are roads wherein the Saviour walketh. Let the righteous be thy constant company, for such ever bring Him where they come. It is the least thing thou canst do to stand where grace usually dispenseth its favour. Even the beggar writes his petition on the flagstone of a frequented thoroughfare, because he hopeth that among the many passers, some few at least will give him charity; learn from him to offer thy prayers where mercies are known to move in the greatest number, that amid them all there may be one for thee. Keep thy sail up when there is no wind, that when it blows thou mayest not have need to prepare for it; use means when thou seest no grace attending them, for thus wilt thou be in the way when grace comes. Better go fifty times and gain nothing, than lose one good opportunity. If the angel stir not the pool, yet lie there still, for it may be the moment when thou leavest, it will be the season of his descending.

Think it not possible to pray too frequently; but at morning, at noon, and at eventide lift up thy soul unto God. Let not despondency stop the the voice of thy supplication, for He who heareth the young ravens when they cry, will in due time listen to the trembling words of thy desire. Give Him no rest until He hear thee; like the importunate widow, be thou always at the heels of the great One; give not up because the past has proved apparently fruitless; remember Jericho stood firm for six days, but yet when they gave an exceeding great shout, it fell flat to the ground. " Arise, cry out in the night : in the beginning of the watches pour out thine heart like water before the face of the Lord. Let tears run down like a river day and night : give thyself no rest; let not the apple of thine eye cease." Let groans, and sighs, and vows keep up perpetual assault at heaven's doors.

> " Heav'n's never deaf,
> But when man's heart is dumb."

There is not a single promise which, if followed up, will not lead thee to the Lord. He is the centre of the circle, and the promises, like radii, all meet in Him, and thence become Yea and Amen.

As the streams run to the ocean, so do all the sweet words of Jesus tend to Himself: launch thy barque upon any one of them, and it shall bear thee onward to the broad sea of His love.

The sure words of Scripture are the footsteps of Jesus imprinted on the soil of mercy—follow the track and find Him. The promises are cards of admission not only to the throne, the mercy-seat, and the audience-chamber, but to the very heart of Jesus. Look aloft to the sky of Revelation, and thou wilt yet find a constellation of promises which shall guide thine eye to the Star of Bethlehem. Above all, cry aloud when thou readest a promise— "Remember Thy word unto Thy servant, on which Thou hast caused me to hope."

From " The Saint and his Saviour."

SLEEP ON, BELOVED!

—o—

SLEEP on, belovèd, sleep, and take thy rest ;
Lay down thy head upon thy Saviour's breast :
We love thee well ; but Jesus loves thee best—
     Good-night !

Until the shadows from this earth are cast ;
Until He gathers in His sheaves at last ;
Until the twilight gloom is overpast—
     Good-night !

Until the Easter glory lights the skies ;
Until the dead in Jesus shall arise,
And He shall come ; but not in lowly guise—
     Good-night !

Only "good-night," belovèd—not "farewell !"
A little while, and all His saints shall dwell
In hallowed union, indivisible—
     Good-night !

Until we meet again before His throne,
Clothed in the spotless robe He gives His own,
Until we know even as we are known—
     Good-night.!